Trophy Elk Hunters

Volume One

STORIES COMPILED FROM

EASTMANS'™

HUNTING JOURNAL

© 1997 The Eastmans' Journal
Cover photo by Michael H. Francis
Illustrations by Chris Lacey, Guy Eastman,
and Tom High

ISBN 1-56037-129-3
First printing November 1998
Second printing March 1999

Printed in Canada.

EASTMANS'™
HUNTING JOURNAL
P.O. Box 5865 • Helena, MT 59604

INTRODUCTION

Over the years *The Journal* has collected many good elk stories. Since most of the magazines now are out of print, this is the second best way to present these stories to our members. Even though these stories are from past issues, they never seem to get old. A good story is always a good story.

Each one has practical information on elk hunting that everyone can use. All the stories are by hunters who love to hunt elk. They are not professional writers—just excellent hunters.

Many of these stories have already become classics. By including them in this book, it will allow you to add them to the reference materials in your hunting library.

CONTENTS

Photo by Alan Sinner

CONTENTS

Photo by Alan Sinner

ARIZONA

The giant Arizona bull has a net score of 427 1/8 B&C.

#3 NONTYPICAL ELK

BY ROGER SELNER

Arizona has produced another giant bull elk! The huge antlers were officially scored at 427 1/8 by B&C measurer Robin Bechtel. The rack has an extra non-matching point on the right antler, making it nontypical.

If the extra point was also present on the left antler, the bull would score over 442 typical, possibly a new world record. This would be an entry score and would have to be panel-measured to determine the final score. Any trophy ranking in the top 10 is required to be measured by a panel of judges.

Tim Pender, the wildlife manager for Arizona Game and Fish Department Region III, was accompanying his 14 year-old son, Tommy, on an elk hunt in Coconino County. On the fifth day of their hunt the Penders found the dead bull. The carcass was completely cleaned, indicating the bull had been dead for several months. After studying the carcass for some time, the cause of death could not be determined. "If this bull lost a fight with a bigger one, I sure would like to see the winner!" Tim remarked.

A short time later, Tommy got his first elk. The Penders then had two trophies to pack out.

DATA ON THE BULL:
Gross nontypical score—436 5/8.
Net nontypical score—427 1/8.
Age—8 1/2 years.
Outside measurement—51 1/8 in.
Inside measurement—50 3/8 in.
Right main beam—59 2/8 in.
Left main beam—57 7/8 in.
Right side—7 points.
Left side—6 points.
Circumference of bases—Right-10 6/8 in.; left 9 7/8 inches.
Royal points—Right—26 5/8 in.; left—26 0/8 in.

Duwane, center, poses with two satisfied elk hunters.

Arizona Big Game Hunts

By Lance Stapleton

In the hunting industry, there are a few outfitters who stand out above the rest. Duwane Adams, owner of Arizona Big Game Hunts in San Manuel, Arizona, is one who does.

I first heard about Duwane years ago while in search of a big Coues deer. Friend and fellow writer Craig Boddington was quick to recommend Duwane as the best guide he knew for Coues deer. I can't even remember why I didn't go that year, but I couldn't forget Craig's suggestion.

When Mike Eastman asked me for names of outfitters who not only consistently produce trophies for their clients but also offer something unique for our readers, I included Duwane on my short list.

If you were to ask Duwane what his secret is, he would quickly say, "You have to see a trophy before you can kill it!"

That's where he shines. Duwane and his guides have brought the art of glassing to a new level, using powerful 15x60 Zeiss binoculars.

The use of powerful binoculars is gaining in popularity throughout the West. Several friends and guides swear by this technique. These big binoculars are expensive, but according to these people, the binoculars are worth the extra money.

One word of advice…don't attempt to set a high power glass on a flimsy tripod—the magnified movement will cause problems.

Duwane is not satisfied to just look at the ridge in front of him, instead he is often looking up to several miles ahead. If you think about it, this makes sense.

First, I don't care how good a shape you're in, I can cover more country with my eyes than you can walk!

Second, if I can spot a buck and watch until he beds, I will have a better chance to stalk and kill him.

Third, I lessen my chances for blundering into a buck by staying as inconspicuous as possible.

Finally, the more time you spend glassing, the more chance you have for some buck to stand up and stretch, to come up over a ridge as the sun changes position or to step out into the open to get a mid-day snack.

Duwane has prepared a video where he and his guides share their hunting tips and secrets on the art of glassing. You can buy one directly from him. Duwane also offers a free marketing video for prospective clients.

Another thing Duwane stresses is where to look. Trophies are normally confined to a relatively small part of your hunting area. He concentrates his efforts on specific areas of a mountain, depending on the time of day, rather than looking over unproductive areas.

Do all of these special techniques produce results? I'll give you an overview.

First, Duwane has guided clients to 12 B&C Coues deer and to two that rank in the top 20 of P&Y.

He personally has collected five bucks that score over 100 points. His personal best Coues buck scored 130 B&C points. His clients' best buck scored 122 points.

He has also produced 10 mule deer bucks for his clients that green-scored over 200 points. . . including several this big from the Kaibab! His clients' biggest nontypical buck green-scored 231 B&C and the best typical scored 211 B&C.

Duwane gets few opportunities to hunt sheep and antelope due to the difficult drawing odds in Arizona. Still, his clients have placed three desert bighorn rams in the book.

He also hunts elk, where he relies largely on bugling or sitting over water tanks. Duwane has produced bulls for clients that scored up to 377 B&C points.

Duwane's hunts are very reasonably priced. While hunting with Duwane, it is not uncommon to have two guides with a hunter to maximize the odds of taking a big trophy. When one hunter fills out, his guide will often pitch in to help another guide.

It's one thing to hunt where trophies are available, it's entirely another matter to find them consistently for clients, and then to get the hunter into position for the kill. Duwane Adams just does it better than some other outfitters.

(**Notes:** *For more information, contact Duwane Adams, Arizona Big Game Hunts, 204 Avenue B, San Manuel, AZ 85631, Ph. (602) 385-4995.*)

THREE FOR THE BOOK

BY ROBIN W. BECHTEL

Nowhere will you find the quality of public land elk that live in Arizona. There isn't a unit in the state that doesn't have the potential of yielding a record book bull.

In 1993, the new #1 Pope & Young nontypical that net-scored 421 7/8 and the new #2 typical that netted out at 398 6/8 P&Y where taken in Arizona. Both of these monster bulls grossed 431 5/8 P&Y. Throw in the 427 1/8 B&C antlers found by Tim Pender that rank as the new #3 B&C nontypical in the world, and you can quickly understand why the record books are being rewritten every year by Arizona bulls.

I've had many *Journal* members ask me which Arizona units offer the best chance of scoring on a record book bull. In my opinion, every unit in the state is above average to excellent when it comes to quality. However, hunting the rut during the early archery, muzzleloader and rifle hunts affords you the best chance of collecting a trophy bull.

Because I do selective trophy guiding, I have been able to help clients and friends put bulls in the record book consistently. Our success has been 100 percent on record book bulls during the Arizona muzzleloader bull hunt.

I have been lucky enough to draw five permits for the early muzzleloader season over the past 12 years. During that time, I have collected five Long Hunter Society (LHS) record book bulls that score 331 0/8 to 357 6/8 from five different units. My good friend, Stan Gaines, has gone two for two scoring on a 355 LHS in 1993 and a 347 6/8 LHS in 1994.

When Stan, *Journal* member John Sievers from Astoria, Oregon, and I drew out for the muzzleloader bull hunt, we were elated. We set a goal of taking three 370-plus bulls. If you set your hunting goals high, it will make you work harder and hunt smarter.

With the muzzleloader hunt scheduled to begin September 23, Stan and I started scouting the first week of August. In 24 days, we located 36 different 320-plus bulls. The weather was hot and dry, so we knew success would be found near isolated water holes and wallows.

I decided to concentrate my efforts on a great area that held many elk

Note the broken G-5 on Robin's bull.

and provided good feed and cover. Dawn was just beginning to break when I first heard the loud bellow of a herd bull accompanied by the sound of cows and calves. I was high in a tree overlooking a large water hole when all hell broke loose. Suddenly, limbs, dirt, mud and water were flying all over the place. Two herds had arrived simultaneously along with their bulls; a 350 6x7 and a one-of-a-kind monster 7x7, 405-plus typical.

The four brow tines on this huge bull extended out to his nose and curled upward. His G3s curved out and up, and when you viewed the bull head on, his six white-tipped tines formed a perfect picket fence, thus I named him "General Picket." His 60- to 61-inch main beams went almost straight up to the G5s and then rolled back.

This bull had G4s and G5s that were all over 24 inches long in addition to 5 1/2- and 7-inch G6s. The only thing keeping this massive bull out of the 420 typical class was his 36-inch inside spread.

Over the next four days, I determined the General followed a definite pattern. On three separate occasions, if I'd had an archery bull permit, I could have arrowed him at less than 25 yards.

Journal *member John Sievers with "Old Warrior."*

By the time John Sievers arrived on September 21, the bulls were becoming more aggressive toward each other. The increasing number of satellite bulls would soon present a great challenge to the General.

The plan was set for opening morning. General Picket would feed with his herd until 6:45 a.m. and then bring them up Picket's draw to bed down in the thick juniper pinion pocket above the feeding area. It was along this route we planned to put him to rest.

Thirty minutes before shooting light, the place was alive with the sound of bulls beating up trees and crashing antlers. Come on, light! At 6:15 a.m., I had just enough light to pick up the General. Unbelievably he was 600 yards west of his usual feeding area. My worse fear became a reality when two, 340-plus, satellite bulls took his cows and drove them off to places unknown. The General was last seen in hot pursuit. What a heart breaker!

Stan Gaines took his 347 6/8 LHS bull off a water hole.

On the second day of the hunt, I shot a nice 331 bull with a broken G5. The bull was so close when I fired, the muzzle blast burned a 3 1/2-inch circle behind his right shoulder. At that range, the bullet didn't have time to expand and the bull went 400 yards before expiring. Stan took his 347 6/8 LHS bull from a water hole that evening.

John Sievers, an excellent hunter and expert shot, harvested a huge-bodied old 6x5 bull on the fifth day. John's bullet took out the lungs at 145 yards. Even with approximately 13 inches broken off his right G4, John's bull netted 330 3/8 LHS.

Some super bulls, including General Picket, made it through the hunt. I'm optimistic he's still alive and kicking.

Robin's tip: Many subscribers have asked me where they can take their bull for mounting. Cape slippage is always a problem when it's hot. Richard Owens at Hunter Lair Taxidermy in Pinetop, AZ, (602) 537-4408, is an excellent taxidermist who will treat you right.

(**Notes:** *Robin may be reached by writing to Bechtel's Big Game Guiding Service, 659 E. Washington Ave., Gilbert, AZ 85234.*)

447 B&C ELK ANTLERS

BY ALAN ELLSWORTH

Growing up in Arizona has given me the opportunity to hunt since I was 14 years old. Now, there is nothing I enjoy more than archery elk hunting during the rut. Besides hunting for myself in the fall, I also work with outfitter Steve Clonts of Black River Guides and Outfitters in Eager, Arizona.

I have been dealing in antlers since the spring of 1990 when I spent two weekends looking for sheds. When I returned home, not only did I have lasting memories and further knowledge of the area, but extra money as well. In a sense, I got paid to walk in the woods. Great!

In 1991, I personally picked up about 2000 pounds of antlers and also started buying antlers from others. This business is very enjoyable, and has allowed me to meet other hunters from all over the country.

Both main beams on Alan's bull are over 55 inches in length.

One of my personal goals as a buyer has been to own an elk rack that would net over 400 B&C points. At the end of February 1995, I was fortunate enough to be in the right place at the right time to make this dream come true.

I was pulling onto main street in Show Low, Arizona, when a truck drove past with a washer, dryer and an awesome elk rack in the back. When the driver pulled over at a local restaurant, I followed him into the parking lot to get a better look at the antlers.

Being an elk hunter I asked, "Where did that bull come from?"

"Kaibab Forest," was his response. After some negotiating, I purchased the antlers. The man I bought them from didn't know when the elk was killed, only that his nephew, who is now deceased, had harvest-

Alan Ellsworth with his giant 447 7/8 B&C Arizona elk antlers.

ed the bull. Earlier that day, the man had picked up the rack in Globe, Arizona where it had been stored in a garage for the last 10 years.

I rushed home and very quickly scored the rack at about 440 B&C net. (I am not an official scorer.) When I returned from work that night, I measured it again more carefully and came up with a score of 446 B&C net. Later that week, Robin Bechtel, an official measurer, scored the rack a 447 7/8 B&C net.

The Arizona Wildlife Trophies Committee panel-scored the rack at 446 2/8 B&C net typical, making it the new Arizona state record.

Notes: If you are interested in buying or selling antlers, you can contact: Antlers Southwest, Attn: Alan Ellsworth, P.O. Box 78, Show Low, AZ 85901, (520) 537-4192.

DATA ON ANTLERS:

Length of points	Right	Left
First	23 2/8	26 7/8
Second	29 1/8	25 6/8
Third	22 4/8	23 4/8
Fourth	24 1/8	22 1/8
Fifth	19 4/8	17 6/8

SMALLEST CIRCUMFERENCES BETWEEN:

	Right	Left
First & second points	11 1/8	10 2/8
Second and third points	8 0/8	7 6/8
Third and fourth points	8 2/8	8 5/8
Fourth and fifth points	6 5/8	8 0/8
Length of main beams:	56 7/8	55 6/8

COLORADO

George's '92 Colorado bull scored 341 6/8 B&C.

MONSTER BULLS AND BUCKS OF RICARDO

BY GEORGE COOK

As my flight came to dock at the Denver airport, my mind came to grips with the realization I was returning to the Ranches of Ricardo, an elk hunter's Shangri-la. Fifteen months earlier I had hunted this fabled ground and collected a world-class nontypical bull. Eight sweeping points adorned the typical right side, with three oddly shaped points on the left. Had both sides matched, the Boone and Crockett score would have been over the 400 mark.

The Hill Ranch provided this 189 2/8 B&C buck for George.

Guides Pat Lancaster and Tim Cudney picked me up at the airport. A four and one-half-hour drive south put us at ranch headquarters where temperatures were unseasonably warm for early December.

Bobby Hill's Ricardo Ranch is a Ranching for Wildlife property, a unique hunting and wildlife management program developed by the Colorado Division of Wildlife. It is a cooperative effort between landowners and the Division of Wildlife that encourages landowners who qualify to practice conservation and habitat improvement. This offers them the opportunity to become more actively involved in the management of public wildlife.

George poses with his 8x3 nontypical bull.

The Division allocates hunting permits to landowners on the basis of herd composition. Landowners are assured a share of allocated ranch permits, with a percentage going to the public through state drawings. Landowners, through Division guidelines, set their own hunting seasons.

At dusk, fellow hunters Tom and David Fines from Mississippi arrived. Pat provided us with a run down on the hunt that had taken place the previous week. Both elk hunters scored, one taking an impressive 6x6 that went 338 B&C. The mule deer hunter took a nice 4x4 buck with an unusual drop-tine.

At daybreak on the first morning, mild temperatures greeted us in the high country but several snowdrifts reminded us of winter's teetering grip. We glassed the timbered ridges, oak brush-covered slopes and beautiful natural burns that make up a portion of the lower ranch. Our morning efforts were rewarded with sightings of three bulls, one of which was an up-and-coming 6-point.

Lunch time found us face to face with an elated Dave and Tom. Dave, who was hunting with guide Mike Powell, had made a trio of 300-yard shots to connect on a gorgeous 7x6 bull that scored 328 1/8 B&C.

The afternoon hunt consisted of a visit to an area known as the Red Hills. After chaining all four wheels, we successfully trail-blazed our way to the 8500-foot level of the ranch. A short hike put us in position to do some extended glassing over more spectacular country.

Before long, Tim spotted three bulls. Pat added eight more as he nestled in for a detailed look. Five of the bulls were 6x6s, including one that would score nearly 310. Yet none were good enough to keep pace with the 325 B&C ranch average.

Soon our attention shifted to a distant 300 plus, 6-point bull. Limited daylight, coupled with a long stalk, prevented a closer look. Two ridges over, three additional bulls fed among the scattered pines. As if this wasn't enough, two 4x4 bucks emerged just 200 yards away.

Day two began with a shrieking 4:15 a.m. alarm. As I fumbled to shut off my morning nemesis, I noticed several shapes outside the cabin window. There, a mere 50 feet away, 17 cow elk and one lone spike fed in the fading moonlight. Even from the comfort of camp, the morning was off to a fast start.

New-fallen snow meant chaining up under the cold cloak of darkness. Again, we headed into the high country where bulls were many and ease of breath absent.

Pat felt with all the bulls still up high, we were bound to find one that would score 320 plus. His prediction materialized minutes later in the form of two huge 6x6 bulls, one a robust 50-inches wide. As luck would have it, these bulls were on safe ground just outside the Hill Ranch property.

Parking at the lower end of Fish Creek, we hiked up to the lower ridges of the Red Hills. Spying through my 10x50 Swarovskis, I quickly found two 6x6 bulls and a single 5x5. Nearby, a heavy 4x3 mule deer pursued several does. We decided to skirt them and take a look into Ricardo Creek, the next drainage over. The Fish and Ricardo Creek drainages work as a natural funnel for bulls coming off the high country. They are major travel corridors for late season bulls.

The wait was a short one as moments later Pat spotted a huge bull 100 yards away. The massive 6-point fed along with a welterweight 5x5. Settling in, my first shot struck a bit high in the lung area. A follow-up shot put the 341 6/8 B&C bull on the ground. After an extended back-slappin', hand-shakin', photo-snappin' session, the work began in earnest.

Back at camp, tales of monster bulls were everywhere. Tom Fine with guide Mike Powell had put together an "almost" stalk on a world-class bull that Mike estimated at 350 B&C.

After lunch, Tim, Pat and I began the skinning chore at the hanging shed out back near a draw. Suddenly, Tim spotted a buck not far away. It took a second statement, lined with choice expletives, to pull Pat and I out of our "doubting Thomas" state. Backing up a step, I caught a fleeting glimpse of a wide-bodied buck and the scramble was on. Grabbing our rifles, binoculars and a single spotting scope, we began our new-found assault from the backyard.

A quarter mile up the draw, threatening skies began what would soon be an extended snowstorm. We carefully searched the hillsides, but Mr. Mulie had simply melted into the scenery.

By 5:00 p.m., four inches of new snow had blanketed the ground. Tom, David and Mike stumbled in an hour later, blizzard weary. Their day's tally of bulls spotted totaled 15. A pork rib dinner hit the spot and brought a most successful and fascinating day to a close.

The next morning it was still snowing as we witnessed the accumulation of 16 continuous hours of snowfall. Pat, Tim and I checked out various nooks and crannies on the lower ranch, spotting five bucks, a scattering of does and a few elk. Everything was still hunkered down.

By 3:30 p.m. the storm had subsided to intermittent flurries and conditions were ideal. Pat suggested we check out a place called Sowbelly Burn where Tim had collected a 188 typical mule deer during a hunt the previous December.

Looking into the burn from a distant ridge revealed five mule deer bucks, one of which was definitely worth a closer look. Pat was already engulfed in the search for a stalking route.

The half-mile stalk was for the most part a downhill affair. Wind direction was nearly perfect with a slight cross breeze as we made our way toward the herd. We crawled up a ridge and peeked over the crest. There stood five bucks. Instantly, my 10x50s were up. At the sight of the biggest buck, I dropped the bi-pod and set up my 7mm Weatherby. The shooter was now ready for business.

At 150 yards the massive buck offered only a quartering-away shot. Centering the cross hairs, I squeezed off a picture-perfect shot. The big 4x4 featured exceptional tine length and mass with a gross typical score of 189 2/8 B&C.

The fourth morning found us headed back to the high ranch with Tom Fines who had two days left to collect a good bull. Pat and I would serve as additional spotters.

From our perch on the southern ridge of the Red Hills, we were treated to a rare sight as a 6x5 180-class buck squared off with a larger-bodied 150-range 4x4. In the wings awaited several does. The scheduled 12-round bout lasted just seconds as the 4x4 scored a quick TKO.

Soon our attention turned to a group of eight bulls roughly 700 yards away. Six were 6x6s, with two scoring around 300 B&C. Quickly a game plan was formulated, and Mike, along with a hopeful Tom and Dave, were off in hot pursuit.

As darkness closed in all too quickly, the stalk went sour and the best bulls fed out of shooting range.

On the fifth morning, Tom took a crack at a 310 class 6x6, but as luck would have it, the volley of shots from his .338 did not find their mark.

As for me, my ship had come in and I returned with a great bull and buck to boot.

*(**Note:** Outfitter Bobby Hill can be reached at (254) 897-7881. Rte. 1, Box 238C, Glen Rose, TX 76043*

BOB VISEK: FIVE YEARS, FOUR SIX-POINT BULLS

Bob Visek lives in Grand Junction, Colorado. Several years ago, he sold his business and now spends the entire Colorado bow season hunting big bull elk. I first learned about Bob's incredible hunting ability while looking through trophy photos at Red Rock Archery in Grand Junction. Bob is an instinctive shooter who patronizes Red Rock Archery, using the indoor shooting ranges and discussing elk tactics with other bowhunters. He has been a serious bowhunter for 27 years. In this interview, Bob tells about elk hunting tactics that have worked for him and how he killed a big 6x7 bull.

Bob, can you tell us about your 6x7 bull?
I hadn't seen this bull before the night I killed it, but a friend had seen him in a heavily wooded draw. I had hunted another big, typical 6x6, without getting close enough to get a shot, so I decided to go to another area that hadn't been hunted for a few days.

There was a storm approaching as I heard a bugle from the draw. Sneaking into the draw I came upon a bugling 5x5. He was not the bull I wanted but I soon heard another bugle. I could tell by his strained, raspy voice that this was a big, heavy bull. I backed off the small one and dropped down low, getting my scent below him.

As I approached the big bull, he was taking cows out of the dark timber into some aspens. I followed close behind, hoping for an opportunity.

As it got darker and began to lightning, they turned back toward the timber. I knelt and waited. When they got within about 40 yards, the big bull stopped and bugled. I hit him with a perfect broadside shot and he went only 75 yards before going down. The score on my bull is 293 2/8 P&Y.

What kind of bow do you use?
I shot my big bull with an Onieda, but this year I'm using a Darton

because I like its new wooden handle. I shoot instinctively with three fingers under the knock, lining my arrow up with the animal's chest cavity. Most elk I've killed have been within 10 to 15 yards. In fact, three of them have been within 12 yards.

How do you get so close?

I let them do the bugling and slip into the herd, trying to get as close as I can. If an elk sees me, I stop and freeze. Nine times out of 10, he accepts me and begins to graze again.

I killed three of my five P&Y bulls in the middle of the day. I start at dawn, just trying to stay with the herd. They are usually moving, feeding, bugling and raising hell. They often move too fast for me to get in front of them, so all I can do is hang back a couple of hundred yards in a kind of buffer zone, letting them move ahead.

When the elk start to bed, I try to get in closer to the bull. The big bull will usually bed down in the middle of the herd while the satellite bulls bed near the edge. I let the big bull bed down, then sneak in as close as possible, usually within 30 to 35 yards of the herd. The satellite bulls will come to the edge of the herd because they get impatient. As soon as one approaches the herd, the big bull will run him off. While the big bull is trying to run off the satellite bulls, I slip between them and the herd. I know he'll come back and then I've got him.

How do you handle the changing wind direction when you are so close?

In the morning, winds are basically stable so I try to stay below the herd and get into position. Often a bull will stop and fight brush, so I try to slip in on him. I stay parallel with the herd at the same elevation, then I don't have to worry about the wind changing. When the temperature rises and the air currents come up the canyons, I try to come in from the top. In the early morning or late evening, I always try to stay below the animal.

Another trick I use is to wear a chamois-colored (buckskin) shirt under my coveralls. If an elk spots me, sometimes I take off the top of my coveralls. Since I am then the same color as they are, the elk aren't so alarmed. If I'm not wearing a chamois shirt, I sometimes just pull the top of my coveralls down to the bare skin. It's a radical way of hunting, but it works for me.

Crawling seems to disturb the animals less than standing upright. If an elk is coming toward me, I kneel down in position on one knee with my black bow in front of my face. I seldom use camo paint, but I do have a baseball-type camo cap with a head net that I pull down to block my face.

It's important to get in front of an obstacle such as a bush or tree, instead of behind it, using that obstacle to block your silhouette. I get between a bull and a cow, kneel in position, and when the bull walks past me behind the tree, I come to a full draw. That way, he doesn't pick out the movement. As soon as he steps out broadside, I shoot.

Do you prefer hunting elk over other animals?

I think an elk is the easiest animal to hunt and mule deer are the most difficult, but there is something special about elk when they are bugling. There is nothing like it in the world. The difficulty in elk hunting comes when you pick out and go after a particular bull, then you'll learn a lot about elk and have a tremendous time.

What part of the day is most successful for you?

Most of the time, I go prepared to stay out all day. Frequently, I am in a good position to kill a bull in the middle of the day when most hunters are back in camp taking a nap. If the hunting is good, you should be out there taking advantage of it. Elk don't stay bedded in one area. When the sun moves, they move. Sometimes they even bed in open areas and if you are back in camp, you won't know these things.

What are some specific hunting techniques that work for you?

I scrape a tree to get a bull really excited. If I do that or bugle, they can pinpoint my location. Then, I move up a ways and get into position where the animal will come in. Most of the time big bulls come in silently but you have to be aggressive and move toward the elk. Don't expect them to come to you. The more aggressive I am, the better I do.

Covering a lot of country is important. Keep moving. The more country you cover, the better chance you have.

Do you have any particular arrow you like best?

I'm a firm believer in a good XX75 arrow because they are extremely durable. I've tried many broadheads, killing most of my trophies with Bear Razor Heads. Several years ago, however, I started using Thunderheads. They are expensive but extremely durable. I've made bad shots and still had tremendous results with it.

Some people dislike bowhunting; what are your feelings?

It bothers me when people talk about how ineffective arrows are.

31

Any animal will be down in eight to 10 seconds with a good double-bladed head. They faint from loss of blood. We've shown bears on video that run as hard as they can after being shot and don't make it 60 yards before they pass out. In 10 to 12 seconds, they are dead. I think a well-placed sharp broadhead is the most effective and humane way to hunt. The recovery rate for animals that have been hit and not killed is tremendous, because with a good sharp broadhead there isn't a lot of tissue damage. The sharper the blade, the more the animal bleeds. Death comes more quickly.

I'm a big believer in bowhunter education. Many people think it isn't necessary, but I think every bowhunter should be required to take the National Bowhunter Education Course. It teaches many things such as the importance of waiting 30 minutes after the shot before tracking your game.

Bugling after you hit the bull is unusual; can you explain why you do it?

As soon as I hit an elk and it takes off, I bugle. Two separate elk I've hit took off, running 60 to 70 yards from me. When I bugled, they stopped and actually walked back toward me. Then all of a sudden, their back legs went out from under them and down they went. Bugling after the shot saves following a lot of blood trail and it calms the elk down after the arrow hits. He knows something has happened but isn't sure what. Curiosity often brings them back to find out just what happened.

I like to hunt an area with a lot of bulls that are talking back and forth but I seldom bugle. I simply go into an area and listen. If I don't hear a bugle, I may give one just to get them started, but once they start bugling, I don't bugle again. I go right to the bull that is bugling.

I see you use fairly large optics.

I use 15x80 Steiner binoculars. They're tremendously effective when the light changes suddenly such as on partly cloudy days. I also carry a small pair of 8x30s. I study an elk or deer a long time before I decide to do anything about it.

Do you carry anything unique in your pack?

In my pack I carry a little device made by a friend of mine. It's a small, round, flat piece of plastic about the size of a silver dollar with three holes to stick your arrows in bored at an angle. There is a 1/4-inch cap with the same threads as on my camera in the top of it. I carry it as a tripod for my little camera that has a self-timer on it, because 99 percent of the time I hunt by myself.

I also carry two or three small squeeze butter jars full of water. When I get thirsty, I drink one full jar. That way I don't have partial jars of water sloshing around in my pack. They are very durable and work well.

What type of clothing works best for you?
My clothes are nothing special but I do try to keep them clean. If possible, I change twice a day. My coveralls have been washed so many times they are quiet and look like something you'd pick up off a hobo. I don't think camo is as important in elk hunting as in other types of trophy hunting. I would like to be able to wear wool clothes, but wool makes me itch. If I could find a little lighter grade of it, I'd wear it more often.

I used to slip my boots off when I crawled into a herd of elk, but when they got up and moved, my boots were back several hundred yards where I started. Once I had a terrible time finding them, so I quit doing that. It isn't a bad idea to carry a pair of sheepskin moccasins for stalking.

This 316 gross bull was taken by Fred Karsten on his Colorado ranch.

Brian Karsten took this archery bull that grosses 348 P&Y.

FATHER & SON ELK STALKERS

Fred Karsten and his son, Brian, are successful archery hunters from Grand Junction, Colorado. Although they hunt several species, Fred and Brian concentrate mainly on bull elk. The majority of their bulls have been harvested near Glade Park, Colorado, where they own part interest in a 3,000-acre ranch.

Their best is an archery bull that Brian took three years ago. It grossed 348 B&C, with a final net score of 329. Fred has also had the opportunity to hunt a monster bull.

After making a good stalk on a small herd, Fred spotted the ivory tips of a bull coming through the oak brush with a bunch of cows. He just knew it was the big bull he had been hunting. When the bull stepped into view, Fred took him.

Now Fred refers to that elk as his "Geek" bull because the trophy had six beautiful points on one side but only three on the other!

Hunting on the Karstens' ranch can be difficult. Quakies and plenty of oak brush make it difficult to use spot and stalk methods.

Fred and Brian have found bugling for elk does more harm than good. There are so many bulls on the ranch that bugling causes them to move away from a potential challenger. It is more productive to sneak through the brush and timber using cow calls. If a bull bugles while they are working the brush, they are often in a good position for a stalk.

In past years their area held a good population of mule deer, but the elk population increased so dramatically that most of the deer have been pushed off the ranch. Although Fred misses the good mule deer hunting, he doesn't complain about too many elk!

The ranch also supports a healthy population of black bear. Before the current restrictive bear hunting laws were enacted, Fred and Brian enjoyed baiting for bears. They would often film each other hunting with archery equipment.

The Karstens use Darton bows and Easton aluminum shafts tipped with Thunderhead broadheads. They also believe in using full camo.

Although Fred's interests lie strictly in the hunting aspect of archery, Brian competes in many tournaments and consistently places among the top finishers.

Craig's Colorado bull gross scored 384 4/8 B&C.

FOUR FOR FOUR, HUNT-OF-A-LIFETIME

BY CRAIG KOHLER

Every few minutes, a bugle would break the silence. All we could see were bits and pieces of a herd of 30 elk feeding in an open park. My guide, Mike Lancaster, pointed out three smaller satellite bulls who seemed very nervous about their back trail.

In the blink of an eye, a herd bull burst onto the scene. He began chasing cows from one side of the park to the other with little regard for the other bulls in the group.

With visibility limited to only a few clear openings in the timber, we needed to gain another 75 yards to get a good look at the bull.

Using the trees for cover, we crawled closer. As if on cue, the bull charged in our direction. He stopped, giving me the profile of his rack I was hoping for. The bull was a heavy-antlered 6x7 with ivory tips and long points. A definite shooter!

I don't know if it was the near-darkness or the fact I was hunting in elk Utopia, but I decided to pass on the bull. It was a tough call, but I felt confident I had made the right decision. Even though I was hunting in one of the West's premier elk areas, a 330-plus bull is hard to walk away from.

By the time we reached the truck, I was second-guessing my decision. I turned to Mike and asked, "Was that a mistake?" His reply was, "Never, your first reaction is usually the right one. We'll just have to hunt harder to find a bigger bull."

His easy smile and positive attitude settled me down, allowing me to start thinking about the prospects of bumping into one of those monsters bulls I had read so much about. Little did I know what would be waiting for me down the line.

My hunt began months earlier when I received a call from my good friend and hunting companion, George Cook. George said, "Craig, the first hunt on the Hill Ranch is available for elk and mule deer, we can have the spots if we move fast."

We had waited for these two spots for three years. Not only were these top dates for elk, it would give us the rare chance to hunt mule deer in the velvet with a rifle. After rolling the numbers over in my head for three seconds, I said yes.

Our encounter with the 6x7 took place the second evening of the 5 1/2-day hunt. We had already seen a dozen 6x6 bulls, so passing was all part of the process, or so we thought.

The next two days produced little more than distant bugles with no sightings. "The tide has got to turn," I thought to myself. I was going into my last full day and I hadn't put a dent in the two tags burning a hole in my pocket.

George set high standards on day three with a beautiful 350 B&C bull and a giant 197 B&C velvet mulie. With his tags filled, George and his guide, Pat Lancaster, would now help by scouting other areas for me. They located what sounded like a beautiful 7x7 bull in a large canyon two miles from where we were hunting.

The next morning found Mike and I in the canyon, hoping the big boy hadn't moved off during the night. We scoured the area, but to no avail. Our plan was to spend this last evening watching the canyon until there was an hour of daylight left. If he was a "no show," we'd switch positions to a big burn to the west. As luck would have it, the 7x7 didn't show and we found ourselves settling into the burn for the evening vigil.

Immediately we saw elk! Two small harems in each corner of the burn and another in the timber. We listened as the bull from one harem screamed his challenge to the other. The bull closest to us appeared to be a 6x6 in the 300 B&C class, but when the farther of the two bulls gave us a good profile, we forgot about the first one in a hurry. A closer look through the spotting scope revealed the bull was a huge 8x7, triple brow tine monster, with long baseball bat-like main beams.

By the time we moved into position, only five minutes of shooting light remained. One shot from my .300 and he was mine.

Standing over the bull, he was just as he had appeared in our view through the spotting scope...and then some. His massive main beams and 8x7 frame made up a rack that would gross score 384 4/8 B&C.

George and Pat were waiting when we pulled back into camp at 2:00 a.m. After a quick dinner and reliving the story one more time, we hit the sack for a 5:00 a.m. wake-up call.

Mike decided we would try to fill my mule deer tag before leaving for the airport. As luck would have it, by 10:00 a.m., we had seen eight bucks and were able to connect on a velvet trophy that gross scored 186 6/8.

This was a first class hunt from start to finish and went the way we had dreamed. This truly was elk Utopia with a mule deer kicker.

(Notes: You may contact Bobby Hill at (817) 897-7881 or Pat Lancaster at (303) 646-0254. All photos in this article were taken by Pat Lancaster.)

Record Book Colorado Bull

By Jeff Barber

The first hint of daybreak appeared on the horizon as I stepped from my pickup. Because this was the last day of the Colorado black powder season, only hours remained for me to conquer the bull that had outwitted me for the last two seasons.

Almost three years of failure had taught me much about the crafty old veteran. I had learned I could leave my elk calls in the truck, for they were of no use against this bull. Although he would answer a bugle from a great distance, calling from within a quarter of a mile would only make him round up his cows and push them deep into the dark timber. Never had I caught more than a fleeting glimpse of his massive antlers as he evaporated into the darkness.

I snapped my fanny pack around my waist, grabbed my muzzleloader and headed into the light morning breeze coming out of the west. After walking about 75 yards, I remembered hearing about a bull that had crossed the highway the evening before just east of where my truck was parked. Having seen only two small bulls during the entire season, I decided to change my plan and check it out. Maybe the bull would still be there.

By the time I got back to the truck, I had convinced myself that it was foolish to change my strategy based on what someone had supposedly seen. Even if it was a trophy bull, the chances of him being there 10 hours later were remote at best. I had promised myself to follow the routine that had paid off for me in the past. Though it was the last day of the season, I decided to follow my original game plan and headed back to the west. If nothing else, I would have the wind in my favor and the time needed to reach my prime hunting area before daylight.

As I climbed toward a large meadow at the top of the mountain, I remember the frustration I had sometimes felt during this hunt. The temperatures had remained in the 70s and 80s throughout the season and a star-filled sky told me this day would be no different.

Dry conditions made quiet walking almost impossible. It sounded as if I was walking on a carpet of potato chips. I winced at the sound of each step, but carefully continued to pick my way uphill.

As I approached the upper meadow, I was careful to remain concealed. Peeking around a large evergreen, I was surprised by the sight of a black bear lumbering across the meadow in my direction. The bear was unaware of my presence until it was directly downwind of me. As the bear whirled and vanished into the early morning light, so did my chance of seeing elk in that meadow.

I moved to a heavily timbered ridge where I had been successful in the past. I was following a well-worn game trail just below the top of the ridge when an unfamiliar sound halted me in my tracks. Something was making a glunking noise just above me. Although it was a new sound to me, I sensed it was a bull elk.

As I started my climb, I was paying too much attention to my footing and not enough to what was ahead. A sick feeling came over me as I glanced up the slope and saw a cow elk peering down at me from the top of the ridge. I knew if she spooked, it was all over. We both stood motionless for what seemed an eternity before she turned and walked away.

I sat down for five minutes to let things cool down before resuming the climb. When I heard the glunking noise again, it gave me some reassurance the bull was still there. I couldn't help wondering what I might find at the top. Would it be one of the two small bulls I had passed on the day before or was I destined for a third round with the old veteran?

Reaching the top, I discovered two cows slowly feeding away from me at about 40 yards. Being well hidden I stood still and scanned the area with my binoculars. There were elk everywhere!

The herd had no idea I was there as I carefully searched for the bull. Finally, I caught sight of a large tan form moving through the timber to my right. The outstretched head and overall size told me this was the bull.

I could see only the bottom half of his body as he pushed several of his cows back toward the middle of the herd. I watched for a glimpse of his antlers through each tiny opening in the timber, but it was just too thick. He would have to go another 20 yards before I could finally see what kind of bull he was. I clicked off the safety of my .54 caliber Knight MK-85 and waited.

When he stepped into the opening at 50 yards, I could hardly believe what I was seeing. It was the old bull I had hunted for three years. Before I could raise the gun to my shoulder, he moved just enough to put a large bush between us. I momentarily contemplated a shot

Facing page: Jeff hunted this smart old bull for almost three years.

through the bush, but decided against it. He was still unaware of me and hopefully patience would provide a better shot.

The bull turned and walked directly away from me and my heart sank. I cursed myself for not taking the shot at 50 yards. He was only a few steps from going over the ridge when he stopped at 75 yards and began feeding. The bull moved forward a few steps, then turned slightly toward me.

I wanted a better shot, but knew this might be my best opportunity. I lined the post of my open sights up with a spot behind his front shoulder and squeezed the trigger. Through the smoke I could see the bull stagger, but remain on his feet.

The main beams on Jeff's bull measure 49 3/8 and 53 3/8 inches.

As I pulled the ramrod out to reload, the rest of the herd vanished over the ridge. The bull attempted to follow, but his pace had been slowed by the 435-grain Buffalo bullet. It took two more rounds to put him down, but even then it wasn't over. He thrashed his huge antlers wildly back and forth, snapping dead branches off a fallen log like match sticks. A chill ran through me as I watched the broken pieces fly. I held my breath, hoping it was only branches he was breaking!

Moments later the bull expired. I walked toward him, carefully examining his rack at every step. Although his flailing antlers had broken off branches almost two inches in diameter, they were still fully intact. I did not relax, however, until I had examined each tine individually.

The bull I had hunted for three seasons lay before me in majestic silence. I sat down next to him admiring his ivory tipped tines and long sweeping main beams. He was even bigger than I remembered. I couldn't help reflecting on my good fortune and how lucky I was that I had stuck to my routine.

(Notes: With a gross score of 375 1/8 B&C and a net of 359 7/8, Jeff's trophy is the largest typical elk ever taken with a muzzleloader in Colorado. The bull ranks as the #5 typical in the Longhunter Society Record Book.)

BULLS OF RICARDO

BY BEAU HUDSON

My friend, Billy Brookshire, is an accomplished deer and turkey hunter who comprehends the nuances of the stock markets as well as any of my associates of 25 years in this ego humiliating pursuit. Billy also has a penchant for meticulously chronicling his hunting trips. He has been telling me over the past years about a place of mythical proportions relative to Wapiti. To me, a quality elk hunt in mountainous terrain is as good as it gets. Billy's invitation to go along was all the impetus I needed.

Bill Brookshire and guide Mike Lancaster.

43

Billy, Rich Good, a Georgia Pacific executive, and I flew to Colorado in October, rented a van and drove to the town of Stonewall located along the New Mexico border. I was slightly let down to find out the town was named for a vertical stone wall near there not my ancestor, the hero of the Army of Northern Virginia.

Mike Lancaster, brother of our outfitter, Pat Lancaster, and Mike Powell, ranch foreman, would be our guides for the next week. Rhonda, Pat's wife, would be our cook of gourmet proportions. We were fortunate that Bobby Hill and his wife, Dottie, owners of Ricardo Ranches, were also there for a few days.

We were to hunt the upper ranch, 15,000 acres of classic elk country located at 10,000 feet in the Sangre De Christo mountain range. Oh, by the way, the upper ranch borders the Vermejo Park Ranch, ever heard of that place? The Hills also own a lower ranch of some 54,000 acres near Stonewall/Segundo.

I would be hunting with Mike Powell, Billy with Mike Lancaster and Rich Good with owner and pro tem guide, Bobby Hill. We hunted by driving 4-wheel drive vehicles to certain areas and then proceeding on foot for as long as was necessary. Don't let the 4-wheel drive part infer that there was any part of this hunt that was not strenuous. It can be toned down for those totally out of shape, but if you want the maximum from this hunt, be in condition.

The first afternoon, Mike and I went to the upper parks, an area comprising thousands of acres where I saw at least 10 shootable, 6x6 bulls before dark.

The next day we covered a tremendous amount of territory. I had asked for a demanding hunt and believe me, these folks will accommodate your needs.

When we returned for lunch, we found that Billy had taken a massive, 350-class 7x7 at 300 yards. This was the second 350 bull Billy had seen that morning, in addition to the four other 6x6 bulls that were in sight when he pulled the trigger. Rich Good had also taken a fine 300 B&C bull.

That day, Pat Lancaster arrived from the lower ranch where Mark Streissguth, an accomplished hunter from Washington state, had taken a great 350 bull and a 196 gross B&C mule deer.

At 9:30 the next morning we were sitting on top of the Hogback, a predominate ridge that gave visual and audio access to much of the area. We could hear consistent bugling several miles down the aspen-clad mountain. Mike's comment was that it was a long shot to follow this up...perhaps Rhonda had fresh-made donuts back at the cabin. My response was that I had had far too many donuts in my life and not enough elk.

Beau Hudson with his 350 B&C Colorado bull.

We dropped off the nearly 45-degree slope and began side-slipping around the hill. As we progressed, the herd maintained a consistent distance. We moved, they moved. Three times we almost stumbled into herd stragglers and had to assume the prone position behind logs or boulders. Gratefully, the wind held, blowing in our faces.

Finally, we came to an incredibly beautiful park where a gurgling creek masked our sound as we quietly inserted ourselves into the elk herd. There were five satellite bulls and 30 cows within 20 yards of where I stood behind a large hemlock. The dominant satellite bull was a 325 6x6 with weak number 6s but tremendous body size. He traversed an arc in front of us within easy bow shot (remember, we were rifle hunting) as the other bulls milled about.

Two things then occurred simultaneously. The herd bull, who was 50 yards in the deep timber, moved off with most of the cows and a large 5x5 came trotting down a path toward me. At about 15 yards, he spotted us, did an immediate 180 degree turn and promptly fell flat on his rear end. This story could have ended right there with me a totally satisfied person.

A 224-yard shot dropped Beau's Colorado trophy.

46

That afternoon, we went to the head of the Ricardo Creek drainage, an extremely remote area of the ranch. We climbed for about an hour to a location where beaver had damned a small creek, forming a heavily grassed marshy spot of about five acres. Through the heavy timber, we could hear elk moving about in the bog. Crawling low into the middle of things, we found several bulls feeding. We watched a particularly nice 6x6

A hilltop view of the beautiful Ranches of Ricardo.

from 40 yards and then passed because of its weak sixth points.

Next, we proceeded to the upper meadow called "Hourglass" and spent the rest of the day looking over a group of 15 animals that included several 300-class bulls.

Dawn on the next to the last day of the hunt found Mike and I making our way into Bear Park. We were watching a group of cows grazing in the upper part of the park when suddenly, the herd bull bolted from cover to confront a satellite bull.

As I lay with the .338 resting on a small Douglas fir, Mike didn't have to say anything. It's sort of like when you see a rattlesnake. No one has to say, "There's a rattlesnake!" You know it is a rattlesnake. When you see a big elk, it is the same thing. I waited until the biggest vital part of the elk appeared in a spot between the aspens. At 224 yards, it was all over for the 350 B&C bull.

Chris' bull netted 404 1/8 nontypical LHS points.

WORLD RECORD BLACK POWDER BULL

BY ROGER SELNER

On September 11, opening day of muzzleloader season, Chris White and his hunting buddy, Paul Bianchi, were sitting at a fresh wallow waiting for daylight. In the excitement of the hunt, Chris had forgotten his bugle in the truck. Armed with a coyote call, he squeaked out a call that sounded like a spike bull, then followed with some cow calls. Immediately a bull responded, and for the next 90 minutes Chris worked the as yet unseen bull.

Finally, Chris saw just enough antler to know it was a legal bull. When the elk closed to within 50 yards, the hunter fired one shot from his CVA Frontier rifle loaded with a 490-grain patched round ball. The shot was good and Chris' trophy went only a short distance before lying down.

Buck fever set in and Chris began to shake as he approached the giant bull. The huge 9x7 would later be officially scored at 404 1/8 non-typical, a new world record for black powder.

Unknown to Chris, his neighbors, Jeff and Becky Barber, had photographed and video-taped the big bull the previous year. Jeff, who took the new state record typical black powder elk had also hunted Chris' bull.

In February, at the International Sportsmen's Exposition in Denver, both trophies were on display in the *Eastmans' Journal* elk display. The two hunters met there for the first time and started swapping stories. Jeff and Chris had a great time sharing their stories with those who stopped by the booth.

After studying the live photos of Chris' bull, I think he would have scored about the same as when harvested. He had longer brow points, shorter royal points and one less nontypical point that year.

See data on bull—next page ⟶

Becky Barber took this photo of Chris' bull the year before it was harvested.

DATA ON BULL
Age: 12-14 years
Hunter: Chris White
Location Taken: Jefferson County, CO
Gross score: 417 6/8 LHS
Net score: 404 1/8 LHS nontypical
Outside Spread: 40 6/8 in.
Inside Spread: 37 2/8 in.

Antlers:	Right	Left
Beams:	51 6/8 in.	52 5/8 in.
Points:	7	9
Circ of bases:	9 7/8 in.	10 1/8 in.

COLORADO TROPHY HUNTER

BY BRIAN MONDRAGON

I guess you could say I've been a lifelong hunter. When I was six years old, I remember going to Grandma's house with my B.B. gun and shooting everything in sight, including ants, grasshoppers and the real trophy, "The black stink bug!"

Since then, I've grown a little but my love of hunting has never changed. Despite my young age, I have taken some great animals. I have set a lofty goal for myself—three entries in the Boone and Crockett record book. The three species I have chosen for this quest are elk, mule deer and antelope. These animals can all be found in the general vicinity of my hometown.

My 1993 mule deer, that green-scored 206 2/8 B&C typical, was shot on an 80,000-acre private ranch northeast of the small southern Colorado town where I live. During the five days I hunted the ranch prior to taking this trophy, I saw many bucks, but I was holding out for an exceptional animal. While tip-toeing over a small cedar-covered hill, I saw the buck bedded 275 yards away. I knew at a glance he was the class of trophy I was looking for.

Although he hadn't heard me and the wind was calm, the deer knew something was wrong. As the buck rose from his bed and started up a ravine on a slow trot, I dropped to one knee and raised the custom .300 Winchester magnum to my shoulder.

Carefully, I placed the crosshairs just in front of the shoulder and squeezed the trigger, instantly dropping the massive buck to the ground. I ejected the spent cartridge and placed another round into the chamber, but there was no need. The 150-grain Grand Slam bullet had done its job.

My brother, Michael, and friend, Lonny, have been my longtime hunting partners. I attribute as much of my success to them as they do to me for the animals they have taken. I believe having reliable partners has much to do with the outcome of a hunt. Everybody has a different way of thinking and it's good to be able to anticipate your buddies' next move.

Brian hunted with his brother, Michael, to take this 356 B&C bull.

My elk hunting experiences have topped my adventures. There is no feeling in the world like the tingling my whole body feels when hearing the bugle of a bull elk and anticipating the sight of ivory antler tips moving through a golden-colored aspen grove.

My best bull to date, which scored 356 B&C, was taken on a private ranch hunt with my brother. The massive bull gave himself away with a bugle as Michael and I walked down a fence line at dawn on the second day of the first season.

HIGH COUNTRY BULL

BY BILL MCEWEN

This bull, which is my personal best, was taken during the Colorado muzzleloader season on a mid-September hunt. With main beams of 50 and 51 inches and an inside spread of 41 inches, he grosses 330, with a final net score of 322 B&C.

Our hunting took place above 11,000 feet after we packed seven miles into a central Colorado wilderness.

There are few trophies like this in Colorado's general elk hunting areas. The overall hunting pressure is so heavy, I'm amazed that any bulls live to maturity. These big bulls are almost never seen during the rifle seasons. The archery and muzzleloader seasons are the only time you have a chance at them.

Bill's black-powder bull grosses 330 LHS.

Colorado's Taylor Ranch provided this bull for Billy.

CHALLENGE IN THE HIGH COUNTRY

BY BILLY PATTERSON

My elk hunt actually began several years ago when a good friend of mine, Greg Simmons, suggested I try the Taylor Ranch, which is in Colorado's Ranching for Wildlife program. I thought about it for a year or so and finally booked a hunt for September 15, the peak of the rut.

As my plane approached Denver, I could see the snow-capped Rockies sparkling white in the afternoon sun. I met outfitter Steve Packer in Alamosa and by sundown we were back at the ranch.

The first morning, my guide, Steve Free, and I were set up in our hunting area by daylight. After not seeing any elk by mid-morning, we climbed to the top of a long ridge that was covered with sign. One bull had been tearing limbs out of the trees six to eight feet off the ground! We set up right in the middle of this old boy's bedroom and spent the afternoon watching and waiting, but no elk showed.

Steve and I hunted hard over the next several days but failed to find a quality bull. On September 19 we drove to the San Francisco drainage located on the lower end of the ranch. As we moved up the mountain at sunrise, we suddenly heard an enraged bull screaming his anger to the world! There is no describing the bugle of a bull elk. It is a beautiful and wild song that literally makes the hair stand up on the back of my neck.

Steve answered the call and we heard the bull thrash a tree, bugle, thrash again and then the sound of hooves on rocks. We followed the herd for over two hours but the bull refused to leave the security of the timber.

After lunch, we moved down the slope to an old burn where five canyons came to a point in the center. This is where the bull had been playing us, now maybe we could play him.

Choosing a good vantage point, we began our wait. Nothing moved until a little after 6:00 p.m. when a lone bull stepped out of the timber 500 yards away. I could see the long tines, and when he raised his head the back forks were even with his flanks. This was what I had come to Colorado to shoot!

Looking across the picturesque Taylor Ranch.

It seemed like an eternity as the bull slowly closed the distance to 300 yards. The center of his chest was facing me and his head and neck were turned hard left. I put the duplex in the center of his neck, told Steve to cover his ears, and squeezed the trigger.

As the .300 Weatherby roared, the bull dove off the trail into the dark timber. There is that instant of doubt when an animal makes a death run into the timber, but when I saw Steve grinning at me I had the feeling everything was going to be okay.

After waiting a few minutes, we walked to the spot where the bull had stood and found the dirt kicked up but no blood. Moving down the ridge, we picked up the first crimson splash on a white log. After that, there was no doubt the bull could not be far. At that point, I could not keep up with my 24 year-old guide as he vanished into the timber.

Suddenly, I heard a war hoop and Steve yelled, "Here he is!" When I saw my bull lying there, he looked absolutely awesome. The sun was sinking fast, so we quickly took photos and dressed out the elk, returning the following day to pack him out.

I can't say enough for the quality of the elk in this area. I had met the challenge of the high country in a beautiful mountain setting and had a wonderful experience I will never forget.

David adheres to a strict trophy management program on his properties.

OUTFITTER FOCUS

REDD RANCHES, GUIDES & OUTFITTERS, INC.

Redd Ranches is a family owned and managed hunting operation that controls over 45,000 acres of private land in Utah and Colorado. Outfitter and owner, David Redd, reports that he, like many ranchers consider wildlife a valuable resource. A resource that becomes more and more valuable with proper management. Toward that end, Redd Ranches works with their regional biologists and a private land consulting company owned by Ken Clegg from Springerville, Utah. David reports that Ken has been of great help in improving the quality of animals on Redd Ranches' property.

Part of David's Utah property is involved in the Posted Hunting Unit Program. With Ken Clegg's help the outfitter hopes to add another of the family's Utah ranches to this excellent program in the near future.

Another advantage of the Posted Hunting Unit Program and Ranching For Wildlife is the outfitter has a certain number of tags provided him by the state. In turn, he makes these available to his clients which means they don't have to depend on a drawing.

The private land drop camps offered by Redd Ranches are geared toward hunters who like to do their own cooking and hunting. Cabins are provided, in addition to a guide who will show you around the ranch and then check in on you every 2-3 days.

Most of the guided hunts offered are 1 on 1. A limited number of hunters and excellent staff contribute to a high success rate. Guided hunters also stay in nice cabins and are provided with out-of-this-world food including homemade pies and bread.

Note: *For more information, contact: Redd Ranches Guides & Outfitters, David Redd, P.O. Box 2151, Provo, UT 84603, (801) 765-0902. Mobile Phone (801) 368-7572.*

Roger Selner scored Gene's bull at 351 2/8 LHS net.

BUGLING BLACKPOWDER BULLS

BY GENE PEARSON

I knew it was going to be a great hunting year for Ray Hughes and myself. In July, we received our Colorado muzzleloader elk licenses and the next day we learned we had also drawn elk tags for the Black Hills of South Dakota. We had tried to get one of these licenses for years and now we had both in one year!

With the blackpowder season starting in September, we had a lot of work to do. I started by calling my cousin, Brooks Hoven, and a good friend, Matt Burrows, both from the Denver area. They agreed to help us prepare for the hunt.

My wife, Dawn, and I drove to Colorado in August to scope out the area Ray and I would be hunting. After meeting up with Brooks and Matt, we headed for the mountains. Starting our first hike at around 9,000 feet, we took it slow...living 20 miles east of Rapid City, South Dakota, at an elevation of only 2,300 feet, I noticed the thin air right away. From there, we climbed slow and steady to the 12,000-foot range where we saw plenty of elk and lots of beautiful country.

After returning home, it was time to find the best gear available for our upcoming hunt. We had hunted elk before but never with a muzzleloader and never backpacking. Visiting with many friends about muzzleloading, we decided on the Thompson/Center Thunderhawk in .54 caliber, noting its lightweight carbine style and in-line dependability. After much testing we came up with a good load using Pyrodex powder behind the 430-grain T/C Maxi Ball. Though we were amazed at the accuracy of the rifle with this combination, we agreed that 100 yards would be our maximum range for an accurate shot.

We had no idea what the weather would be like in the middle of September, but I did know that quality footwear would be a must. Since I have weak ankles and much of our hunting would be over rocks and steep terrain, I chose Danner boots. The hunt was a tough test for them but they held up well and were quite comfortable.

Matt recommended Abe and Son elk calls, so I gave Abe a call and had a pleasant visit with him. He was very knowledgeable and helpful in answering all of our questions. After receiving our Dominator bull call and the Stimulator cow call, we practiced daily and watched many videos about the rutting habits of elk.

We knew we had to get in the best condition possible, so placing bricks in our backpacks and hiking the steep river breaks near our home, we trained to get in shape. Unfortunately, we had no way of preparing for the high altitude of our hunting area.

Arriving in Colorado the day before the season opened, we met up with Brooks and headed to the huge drainage we planned to hunt. We loaded our packs with enough supplies to hunt three days and hiked nonstop for 1 1/2 hours in order to make camp before dark.

Opening day dawned clear and warm. With Brooks working the calls, Ray and I walked up a slight incline ahead of him. Thirty minutes into the hunt Ray spotted two bulls coming in our direction. As we lay on the hillside, the 4-point and spike bulls were almost to us when suddenly, a squirrel sounded off and spooked them back to the edge of the timber. Watching the smaller bulls, I glanced farther to my left and spotted a monster 5x5 with coal black antlers heading down a game trail right toward us.

With the bull only 50 yards away, I got into a comfortable shooting position. All I could think of was getting a clean lung shot. At 40 yards the bull stopped, faced us for a second, then turned his wide rack and looked behind him. Though I had a clear shot at his chest, I chose to wait, hoping he would turn broadside in response to Brooks' cow calling below us. Just as planned, the bull headed toward the Stimulator cow call, then stopped broadside at 25 yards. The trouble was that he was behind the only tree within 20 yards in any direction, all I needed was one more step for an easy lung shot.

That bull was so close we could see his eyelids blinking, and yet I couldn't get a clean shot. After a few seconds he caught our scent, whirled around like a big buckskin horse and headed for the thick timber. When the bull stopped at the edge of the trees 70 yards away, I took aim and fired. Even as I squeezed the trigger, I somehow knew it was a clean miss. We searched for signs of blood but found none. I was heartbroken knowing the bull of-a-lifetime had been so close, yet I was unable to connect.

Returning to camp, we hunted hard that afternoon and all the next day. However my shooting had spooked the herd, so we started the long three-hour, uphill hike out to the trailhead. With the heavy pack on my back, I began to tire after two hours. I had to keep telling myself to take one more step as I gobbled vitamin C tablets from my pack, hoping to gain enough energy to complete the journey. The high altitude really took its toll, and by the time we finally reached the pickup, I was totally exhausted.

We spent that night in Denver with Brooks' mother, Shirley. The next day we went to another area that Matt and I had scouted earlier. Arriving before daylight, Ray and I went over our topo maps and decided to hunt the edge of a large canyon that had a big meadow in the bottom. We bugled our way through the canyon, but were unable to get a response. It was 10:00 a.m. when we climbed out and headed for the base of a nearby mountain. With the weather being so warm, we figured the elk would be bedded down by then.

Ray and I decided to split up with me taking the lead. Less than 15 minutes later, I heard the sound of Ray's Dominator bull call followed by an immediate answer from a deep-voiced bull. I heard a crash in the timber to my right, and before I knew it a large 6x6 was standing broadside at 30 yards looking back at Ray. I raised the Thunderhawk, aimed behind the front shoulder and fired. When the smoke cleared, the giant bull was still standing as if nothing had happened. I knew I had hit him because some hair was out of place over the lung area, but it was hard to believe he took a 430-grain bullet through the lungs and was still standing.

Soon, however, the bull began to get heavy on his feet. When he tried to jump over a large rock, his front end went down and his rear went over his head, then he lay still. Quickly, I began to reload. With one eye on the bull and the other on the reloading, it's amazing I managed to get any powder down the barrel! Taking a good rest I watched the fallen bull for a minute or so until Ray arrived.

After a photo session, we began to bone out the meat one half at a time.

Gene saw plenty of elk while scouting at 12,000 feet.

61

The bullet had gone through both lungs, coming to rest next to the hide on the opposite side without ruining any meat. I weighed the bullet when we got home and was amazed to find it had retained 100 percent of its original weight.

Since we had left our big packs in Denver, we had only small day packs and game bags for packing the elk out. It took six hours to complete the four trips each that were required to pack out the 420 pounds of meat and the head. The temperature was 90 degrees so we had to quickly find a locker in Denver before the meat spoiled.

Returning early the next morning to find a bull for Ray, we called for quite some time but couldn't get an answer. At 10:30 a. m., we decided to bugle one more time about 200 yards from where I shot my bull. I bugled and got an answer from about half way up the side of a mountain. We hurried toward the area on a dead run. As we drew nearer, I bugled again and got another answer—this time he was very close. I began to rake the trees with a large stick to get the bull excited while Ray continued in the direction of the bugle.

As Ray was going up, the large 5x5 was coming down and they met in the middle. Unfortunately, the elk got behind a tree and Ray couldn't get a clean shot. The bull soon decided he had had enough of us and headed down the mountain into the heavy timber.

When we got back to South Dakota, I had a taxidermist mount my bull European style. He scored it at 353, just short of making the Boone and Crockett Awards Book. At that time I knew nothing of the Longhunters Society, so I thought no more about the score of my bull until several months later when Ray was in Rapid City at the Black Hills Sport Show. There, he met Roger Selner who tours with the *Eastmans' Journal* World Record Elk Tour. While visiting with Roger, Ray mentioned my elk and Roger, who is an official scorer for Pope and Young, Boone and Crockett and the Longhunters Society, asked if he could see the antlers.

I took the head in the following day and had Roger score it. With a gross score of 359, and a final net of 351 2/8 LHS, my bull ranks as the number three typical in Colorado and number seven in the nation.

Later, on our Black Hills hunt, Ray harvested a good 5x5 while I chose a nice spike for quality eating. I believe the Black Hills of South Dakota are a real sleeper for quality bulls.

There are many friends and family who made my year of hunting such a success. First, I thank God for all that happened and for returning us home safely. I also want to thank Brooks and Shirley Hoven and Matt Burrows for their hard work and hospitality. Finally, thank you Ray Hughes for your friendship, support and kindness.

I D A H O

Ron packed in with llamas to take this nice Idaho bull.

Llamas and Muzzleloaders

By Ron Lampers

For four years in a row, I've hunted elk in Idaho with my brother, Don, and nephew, Jason. This year, unlike the past, we packed in with llamas which meant we could maximize our time doing what we came to do, hunt.

We discovered llamas have many advantages over pack horses. No longer did we have to make extra trips to pack in feed. Llamas eat most anything, including pine, cedar and fir boughs, as well as bark. They had no problem getting enough to eat even in two feet of snow. Watering wasn't necessary as they got all the moisture they needed from the snow and vegetation.

We also discovered, as with horses, conditioning your llamas is very important. We began the trip with four llamas but, unfortunately, one wasn't in packing shape. As a result, all the packing was done with three. Nevertheless, the trip was a pleasure.

We loaded our three llamas with 70 to 90-pound packs for the trip into the steep mountains. Periodic stops were required to give them a rest, particularly on the very steep sections of the trail. Llamas cannot keep pace with a horse when going uphill, but they are quieter and much more sure-footed. Llamas are also gregarious and therefore don't like to be separated from each other.

After the first few days of our hunt, we started taking the llamas part way into the hunting area before tying them off for the day. We could tie a llama to the smallest little branch and he would never break it loose.

During the first few days we spotted many bulls, including some 5x5s and two very nice 6x6s. Several attempts were made to stalk them, but we were never able to take a shot.

One morning toward the end of our hunt, we decided to move to an area farther back in the mountains. I was sure we'd see some good bulls because I had always found them there in the past.

At 11:05 a.m., I spotted some cows on a small knoll 600 yards away.

There was a nice 6x6 bull right in the middle of them. That's not what I'd hoped for because it's always more difficult to hide from all those eyes.

After watching the herd bed down, we made our move, staying out of sight and keeping the wind in our favor. At 150 yards from the herd, a nice 4x4 whitetail buck jumped up and stood broadside only 75 yards away. He was very enticing but my sights were set on something bigger.

Shortly, the buck took off and fortunately didn't spook the elk. Slowly and carefully we moved in a little closer. My plan of attack was spoiled when I spotted another bunch of cows between us and the bull. Suddenly, the wind started to shift so we quickly relocated to maintain our advantage.

I had hunted this knob many times before and knew we would have to work our way up through some very thick brush and timber. Two hours later, we found ourselves very close to where I'd last seen the bull.

As I started to move around a tree, I caught a glimpse of a bull looking at me 50 yards away. The only thing preventing him from seeing me was a small tree with a clump of snow on top. The wind was still in our favor, so he couldn't wind us but we had obviously been heard.

I couldn't see his head but I did have a clear shot at his chest. Slowly I drew on him and fired a round through his pump. I knew I had him when I heard that familiar whack from the sound of the .50 caliber hollow point fired from my Hawkins Thompson Center.

Before I approached the bull, I attempted to reload but my ramrod had frozen to the stock. Knowing my nephew had his gun loaded, we moved up to check things out. There was a three-foot wide blood trail in the snow, so following him was going to be easy. When we got to the spot where the blood trail began, Jason said, "There he is, Uncle Ron."

Only 30 yards away stood a 6x6 bull. I knew immediately he wasn't the bull I'd just shot so I told Jason to shoot. Confused, he lifted his gun and aimed at the bull but didn't shoot. Knowing the moment wouldn't last long, I again urged him to shoot. An eternity (8-10 seconds) passed and still he didn't shoot. Finally, the bull wheeled and vanished over the ridge and into the brush.

Afterward I asked him why he didn't shoot. He said he couldn't make up his mind whether to shoot at the neck or behind the front shoulders. This was his first elk hunting trip and I'm sure he'll always recall the moment he could have taken his first big bull.

With a green score of 295 B&C, my bull turned out to be the biggest seen on the trip. The next day we packed the meat on the three llamas, each easily carrying 100-120 pounds. I returned the next day for the cape and horns.

Packing the game out with the llamas was a pleasure compared to past years using horses. The entire trip was made under complete control. Working pack horses up a very steep, snow-covered hillside is always intense. They carelessly dash up and down the slopes with no mind as to where they place their feet. One misplaced step could result in a pileup with you at the bottom.

Llamas do everything gently and calmly. If their front leg happens to hit the back of your foot, you hardly even feel it. Each llama has his own personality. Mine followed me like a shadow. I didn't really need a rope because he was always next to me, looking over my shoulder. When I looked left, he looked left. When I looked right, he looked right. By the end of the trip, the llamas went everywhere we did. They had become part of the gang.

Scott's 6x6 Idaho bull grossed 277 P&Y.

Judd and Scott, along with wrangler, Jason Cleverly, show off the antlers.

IDAHO ARCHERY BULLS

BY SCOTT MACKINTOSH

Our elk dream finally came true last year in Idaho. My brother, Judd, and I have had a passion for bugling elk for some time now. I had taken only two small bulls with my bow and felt I had a lot to gain. Judd had experienced several close calls, but hadn't been able to make the connection he wanted.

When our friend Don White first took us hunting in this area, it seemed like there were so many bulls we couldn't help making it happen. But, as hunting goes, we went home empty-handed.

This year, we vowed, was going to be different. We packed in several miles and had close calls, but couldn't connect on a good bull. Bugling didn't seem to work as there were so many bulls they weren't willing to risk losing their cows in a confrontation.

Since September 19 was my son's seventh birthday, I hoped it would be our day. We saw bears, heard lots of bugling and came close to getting shots at good bulls. About 1:00 p.m., we heard bulls bugling in a canyon and quickly moved into a position where we could get a good look at them. Just as we brought them into focus, their screams stopped. We continued glassing for a while before growing tired and falling asleep in the afternoon sun.

After sleeping for quite some time, we were suddenly awakened by the breathtaking screams of bulls nearby.

Judd decided to make a stalk on a good bull, while I moved into an ambush position just in case his stalk went sour. After half an hour, Judd appeared, saying he'd hit the bull. I was elated but Judd was glum, fearing he had hit the bull too far back.

Our conversation was cut short when two other bulls began screaming not far away. I went in for a stalk, having to go for the smaller bull due to the wind direction. I finally got within range, but had to hold back when several cows fed into the opening between the bull and me. Finally, the bull came out of the timber to gather his herd. A perfect, double-lung shot ended my hunt. I was elated, but my excitement was short-lived by the knowledge that Judd's wounded bull was still out there somewhere.

We took care of my bull, and with a prayer in our hearts, resumed our search for my brother's bull. The blood trail was shaky with little sign and we were forced to give up at dark.

Early the next morning, the search began again. Eight hours later, Judd found his 6x7, 388 gross bull.

If anything could equal that moment it was the honesty displayed by two fellow bow hunters. After searching for two hours, Judd came to the top of a little knoll and gave a short bugle that was answered instantly by another bugle. He proceeded to mew and that too was quickly answered. The replies were so perfect Judd had a feeling it was anther hunter. Sure enough, two hunters soon appeared out of the timber.

After the hellos, Judd asked if they had smelled an elk as they came up the trail. "How long have you been looking for your elk?" Asked the older man.

"A little last night and some this morning," Judd replied.

The man pointed to the timber as he said, "It's over there. We were just sick for the hunter who lost him and hoped he would return."

The men turned out to be Ron Parrish, a former president of the Idaho Bowman's Association, and his son, Lance. They had ridden their horses an hour from camp before tying them up and proceeding on foot. Just 60 yards into the trees they came upon Judd's dead bull. They spent half of their hunting day trying to salvage what they could of the animal just in case no one returned for it.

Ron and Lance were excited to learn this exceptional bull was Judd's first archery elk. Their efforts were made worthwhile knowing that Judd could claim his prize.

Judd and I admire these men who showed such true sportsmanship and let honesty prevail. They sacrificed a half day of their valuable hunting time to help someone they had never met. We all need to be this kind of sportsmen.

We were happy to learn that Lance later took a nice 6-point with his recurve.

TRIPLE SIXES

BY RON LAMPERS

This Idaho elk hunt with good friend, John Jensen, and my nephew, Ryan Lampers, is one I will never forget. Our late-November muzzleloader hunt took place in a remote area we had packed in to using my llamas. Conditions were cold and snowy, and accordingly we came across very few hunters in the area. There was snow on the ground when we arrived at our campsite, and it continued to accumulate until the day we left.

Our first and second days were set aside for hiking in and setting up camp. Llamas do not set a fast pace, but they do a great job of taking the load off your back. Going in, we load them with 60 to 75 pounds, depending on each animal's ability. This year we included a supply of llama pellets to supplement their diet due to the expected severe weather. Although llamas will eat most anything, we have found they do appreciate a little reward after each day's work.

Success came early in our hunt. On our first day out, Ryan headed to an area he had hunted the previous year. John had never hunted this area before, so he came along with me to a different spot. Our progress was slow due to the difficulty of breaking trail in the deep snow.

While making our way through some heavy timber, we came across fresh tracks that were going in our general direction. After a while we noted the tracks looked as if the elk were starting to mill around, so we took our time, carefully scanning the landscape for a big bull. It wasn't long before we got our wish. I spotted a large 6-point standing in the timber and raised my gun, but the bull swiftly moved away before I had a chance to shoot. It was obvious he was not going to let us get close to him so we veered off to look for other elk.

Before long, we found a herd of 30 to 40 that included several bulls.

I glassed them for a while but did not see any that were larger than a 5-point. The elk were completely oblivious of our presence, so we decided to move closer. Ninety minutes later we were right above the herd. We continued to glass for larger bulls but if they were there, we couldn't spot them. The herd was still undisturbed as we exited the scene. When I told John we needed to move on, I could tell he was having a hard time leaving behind a 5x5 that was within range of our muzzleloaders.

It was getting late and we had just enough time to check one more patch of timber before dark. As we moved slowly through the deep snow, I caught a glimpse of antler tips waving in the thick brush. Upon closer inspection, I could see a 6-point bull raking the brush and small pine trees.

Setting the hair-trigger on my Thompson Center .50-caliber Hawkens, I squeezed off a shot. To my surprise the elk simply looked up and seemingly puffed out his chest as he looked around. Unaware of my location, the bull just stood their trying to get a fix on me. Standing in snow up to my waist, I was partially hidden by a large tree. Shocked that somehow I had missed, I motioned for John to take a shot. My partner moved alongside me but couldn't locate the bull in the thick brush. Rather than waste any more time, John quickly handed me his .54-caliber Hawkens.

I fired a shot and this time the bull went down. Because of my angle and the way the bull fell, I knew I had broken its back. I could hear him thrashing around in the brush and I figured he would try to drag himself downhill.

After reloading our rifles, I moved over to where the bull had first fallen, while John took a lower route in case the elk was still moving. As I approached the spot, I could see the bull's trail going downhill. About that time, I heard John yell that he had the bull in front of him.

As we examined my elk we were surprised to find one bullet hole through the back and one just behind the front shoulders. Surprisingly, my first shot struck exactly where I had aimed. Had I taken the time to reload my gun rather than using John's, it is likely the elk would have dropped in its tracks from loss of blood. Then again, had John taken the second shot and unknowingly missed, the elk might have dropped before we could have reloaded, leading us to believe he had shot the elk. In any event we got the elk but clearly things may not always be the way you assume.

We were eager to tell Ryan of our success when we got back to camp late that night. However Ryan had also been successful, bagging an even bigger 6-point bull than mine.

The next couple of days were spent packing the meat out with my llamas. John had several almost-connections with some exceptional bulls and did eventually fill his tag on the sixth day.

MONTANA

Mike harvested this 348 B&C bull on his first trip to the Flying D Ranch.

FLYING D TROPHY HUNT

BY MIKE LOWRIE

After experiencing two great hunts on the Flying D Ranch, I plan to return to this wonderful Montana property every year I am fortunate enough to draw a tag.

There are usually only 12 people in camp during a Flying D hunt: five hunters, five guides, a cook, and the outfitter. This creates more of a hunting camp atmosphere than on some of the other large ranches I have hunted. You have more of an opportunity to get to know your fellow hunters.

After the evening hunt, everyone gathers for drinks or a soda to discuss the day's events. Talk centers around the game seen that day and what is planned for the following day. That's what I really enjoy, the closeness and camaraderie among the hunters.

Immediately upon arrival at the ranch, everyone goes to the range to check their rifles. With all weapons zeroed in, hunters are shown to their cabins.

After lunch, hunters view a slide show of the quality of animals they can expect to harvest, as well as tips on shot placement. Everyone benefits from this great presentation.

Later that afternoon, your guide will drive to a high point from which you can glass. If game is spotted and enough daylight remains, a stalk is attempted. If it is too late in the day, plans are made for the following morning.

I took my best buck on the first evening of my first Flying D hunt. My guide, Bobby, and I were looking at an elk herd from the top of a knoll when I spotted a small herd of deer. We stalked to within 200 yards and I could tell through my 8x Zeis binoculars he was a good buck. I took the 36-inch 7x9 right at dark.

That year, I killed my elk on the fourth morning of the hunt. We found the bull late on the third day of the hunt. Figuring it was too late for a stalk, we made plans to return the next day.

Early the next morning we drove to within a mile of the elk, then continued on foot. We had to slide on our bellies in eight inches of snow to

75

complete the final part of the stalk. I took the best of the four bulls in the herd with my Winchester .300 magnum Model 70. He gross-scored 348 B&C.

During my hunt the following year, I was very particular for the first three days, passing up several bulls in the 330 class. Without weather to push them out of the high country we didn't see as many bulls as the previous year, but on the fourth night I took a good bull that scored 327 B&C.

We spotted the elk at 700 yards, but due to a lack of cover, had to make a two-mile stalk to come in on him. Sprinting the last leg of our stalk, we found the bull was still too far for a good shot. With darkness fast approaching, we finally caught the elk walking away at 300 yards. I hit him with my .300 as he crested the ridge.

It took two hours of searching in the dark before we found my bull. Fortunately, we were able to drive a small 4-wheeler to the elk and drag him out to the pickup.

On the last day of my hunt, I also took a nice 32-inch 6x6 mule deer. The deer hunting was tough that year, so I felt fortunate to take such a good buck.

Mike's comments: The Flying D is just gorgeous! You have everything from high, snow-capped peaks to lush meadows.

The ranch covers over 100,000 acres and is divided into five areas, one for each of the guides. The guides hunt the same areas each year and know every inch of them. My guide grew up on the Flying D and has hunted it for about 20 years.

If a hunter hasn't harvested by the last day, two of the guides will team up to help him fill his tag. Everyone works together to insure the clients have a great hunt.

On a typical day, the morning hunt starts before daylight with everyone returning to camp later for lunch.

The afternoon hunt starts around 2:00 and runs until dark. The outfitter will often drop the hunter and guide off at a high ridge, then pick them up at the bottom.

The way I see it, you get 10 hunts…five in the morning and five in the evening. If you are looking for a quality mule deer and elk hunt, you cannot beat the Flying D.

(**Notes:** *For more information, call the Flying D Ranch at (406) 763-4419.*)

Southwestern Montana Opportunities

By Conrad P. Nussbaumer

For the past three hunting seasons, my friends and I have hunted southwest Montana's Region Three. Ours is a relatively diverse group, ranging from those who would be thrilled to harvest any elk to those who hunt hard for a wallhanger. Our ages range from 24 to 75 years.

We feel Montana's nonresident big game combination package is a very good value and began hunting there after Idaho raised the ante for their nonresident deer and elk tags. Southwest Montana was chosen based on hard data, the advice of friends, and information gathered from outfitters we talked to at the Rocky Mountain Elk Foundation's Elk Camp.

Region Three has a five-year average elk success rate of 27 percent, according to the *Montana Hunting Almanac*. The almanac also reflects several districts in the region where a good percentage of the harvest is 5-point and larger bulls. It was also noted that one third of all the bulls and 40 percent of all Montana elk are harvested in Region Three. These statistics, combined with relatively good access and a high percentage of public lands, lured us to southwest Montana.

Most of those in our group cannot afford the services of an outfitter. Even those of us who can, derive a great deal of satisfaction and pride in fending for ourselves. Cooking, packing lunches, washing dishes, cutting firewood, and field dressing and packing out big game are to us an integral part of the hunting experience that is almost as important as the kill.

We do not have pack animals so we must compete with rank-and-file hunters. A large military tent served as our abode the first two years, but a combination of 10-below-zero temperatures, a very noisy rain fly and the lack of shower facilities convinced us to rent a bunkhouse.

The first year we paid our dues learning the country and the habits of the elk. There were elk hanging in nearby camps and we saw many live elk, but no antlers. We settled for an eating elk that year.

Conrad, left, and John Nussbaumer with John's Montana bull.

We fared much better the second year, taking two cows and a bull. The respectable bull was harvested in his bed by David Fields. We found the bull in the heart of the National Forest with a broken right rear leg that apparently occurred two months earlier during the rut. Dave took some good natured kidding about killing a handicapped bull that needed a crutch. In truth, the bull was very mobile and we were all quite envious. Backtracking the bull from his bed revealed he had been dragging the broken leg in the snow.

Two game wardens magically appeared as we were beginning to skin Dave's bull. They were especially interested in determining the cause of the broken leg, but no evidence of either a bullet or arrow wound was found. We ended up losing that quarter of the elk and the rest was extremely tough, fit only for stew meat by way of the crockpot.

We requested a replacement tag since the carcass was somewhat defective. The wardens agreed, providing we surrender the entire animal. Dave respectfully declined to part with his antlers. The mounted trophy brings back many pleasant memories from its prominent location in Dave's home.

At every ranch where we asked to hunt, permission was granted. We would drive up to the house, introduce ourselves, ask permission to hunt and give them a business card. We killed a cow elk on one of these ranches while another was killed on National Forest land behind a ranch. We express our appreciation by sending each rancher some candy, nuts or fresh fruit the next holiday season.

When arrangements were made to rent this year's bunkhouse, we were told we could cross the ranch to public lands but a $20 per person, per day trespass fee was required to hunt on the ranch. Upon arrival, however, the owner told us he recently enrolled his ranch in the Block Management Program and consequently we, and other hunters could hunt on his land without paying.

We believe this is an excellent program, utilizing license fees to compensate landowners for allowing hunting and feeding wildlife. Our host told us he could carry an additional 100 cows with the feed consumed by elk each year. An aerial survey of his and two adjacent ranches just before the rut revealed over 80 mature bulls in the general area.

This information suggests a good bull/cow ratio which, combined with the harvest data, reflected a very healthy herd. We compliment the landowners and the Montana Department of Fish Wildlife and Parks for an excellent program that appears to be a win-win situation for everyone.

Following the advice of the ranch foreman, my brother, John, downed a nice 6-point bull running in the willows on public land behind the ranch. The distinguishing feature of this bull was the uniformity of his antlers. The local taxidermist liked the rack so much, he agreed to mount it for half price provided he could display it for a year and a half.

We took the next day off to rest, get the cape to the taxidermist and prepare for the remainder of our hunt. Then, we again followed the advice of the foreman and hunted the area between the sagebrush and black timber. It was snowing lightly and the wind was blowing hard. Dave and I each picked up fresh tracks, and by 11:00 a.m. both had elk down. Dave killed a yearling cow while I bagged a fat forked-horn with unusual antlers.

Dave Fields took this bull in 1994.

Two friends from Montana joined us for the second weekend of hunting and harvested a 5-point bull from a clearcut. They saw more fresh sign over the weekend than they normally see during an entire season near their home in the northwestern part of the state.

Our experience suggests that a quality hunt and respectable antlers are still possible without packing into the hinterlands or hiring the services of an outfitter. Researching data that is readily available, combined with contacting wildlife biologists, foresters, ranchers, taxidermists, outfitters and other hunters, will suggest areas where chances are good to excellent. As long as we continue to draw tags, we plan to return to southwestern Montana.

Montana Archery Bull

By Tammy Munis

Though I've taken several big game animals with my rifle, this was my first successful bow hunt. In the past I've worked hard until I was right in among the elk but, unfortunately, things just hadn't worked out.

The day before I took this elk, my husband, Brian, and I were heading toward an area we planned to hunt. We had just stepped out of the pickup when we heard a bull bugle from across the road. After a short discussion, we decided to ignore him and continue with our original plan. That bull bugled the entire time we were hunting. He was really starting to bug us!

The following morning, we returned to the area to see if the bugling bull was still there. Sure enough, we found him in the same meadow as the day before. As he started moving his cows toward the heavy timber, Brian and I split up to follow him. The bull bugled constantly as he moved along.

I had gone about a half mile when I happened to look up. There he was, right above me! I could hear the cows talking as I quickly knelt down in a small clump of jack-pines. I was really excited!

Brian was 50 yards below, going crazy. He could plainly see the elk, but he wasn't packing his bow that day. My husband gave two cow calls, and the bull began moving toward him.

That bull did everything you have ever heard of a bull elk doing. He bugled and grunted while thrashing his antlers and tearing up the ground. He'd move down a few yards, get mad and repeat the performance. I would have given anything for a video camera to record this display.

The bull worked closer and closer toward the sound of Brian's cow call. I came to full draw for what seemed like five minutes. I started to shake with fatigue but was afraid to let off for fear I wouldn't have the strength to draw again. At 10 yards he finally veered to the right, giving me a broadside shot. Concentrating on his vital area, I released.

When my arrow hit, the bull spun and ran downhill 30 yards, then cut uphill for another 20 yards. He suddenly stopped, began to sway, then

Tammy made a 10-yard shot on her Montana bull.

fell over. Brian watched the whole thing.

Tammy's comments: While archery elk hunting, we bugle sparingly only to locate bulls. Bugling doesn't work in this country like it used to. The elk have been tricked by hunters too many times. We like to stay quiet, wait for a bull to bugle, then move in on him. Brian is very successful with his cow call. We also do a lot of pre-scouting to learn where the bulls are living.

I would like to see more management in this area for trophy bulls. We actually have too many elk, the number of cows is just unbelievable. In past years, some tremendous bulls were taken from this area, but now it is extremely rare for a quality bull to be harvested.

We also used to enjoy very good mule deer hunting, but with over-population of elk and mountain lions, the quality of our deer hunting has really gone downhill.

(**Notes:** *Tammy and Brian live near Philipsburg, Montana. Tammy shoots an XI Legend set at 55 pounds. She uses XX75 shafts with Satellite 110-grain broadheads.*)

The big bull came running when Brian cow-called.

Mike's Montana bull netted 361 4/8 B&C.

BACK COUNTRY BULL

BY MIKE RUSSELL

My hunting partner, Neil Craig, and I had experienced an unsuccessful Montana elk because the snows were late in coming and many of the elk didn't migrate until after the season had closed. Considering the low harvest that year, we felt there would be a good carry-over of big bulls for following season. I was elated to receive my Montana tags, but unfortunately, Neil failed to draw.

Since Neil lives close to our hunt area, he agreed to provide me with scouting reports on elk activity as the season neared. By the time I arrived for my hunt, the prospects for an excellent season were definitely in view.

Neil and I drove to my hunting area on November 6. As we began to glass, Neil pointed out a steep draw where he had seen a good bull earlier in the week. We discussed a plan of attack for the next morning and Neil agreed to check with me at noon to see how I was doing.

The following morning after walking by the light of my flashlight for an hour, I was within sight of the steep draws Neil and I had glassed the day before. As it grew light, I began to glass and instantly spotted a good bull feeding in a brush patch just below a timbered ridge.

Dropping down, I was able to get behind a rocky hogback that would conceal my stalk. After a steady two-hour climb, my legs were beginning to cramp up. I was pretty sure I was above the bull, but when I eased out on a rocky ledge to look, he was nowhere to be seen. Moving across to the next hogback, I brought up the binoculars again, but still no elk. My hopes of sneaking up on the big bull as he fed were beginning to fade.

The cold wind was blowing in my face with increasing strength as I stopped to put on a dry longjohn top and fleece vest. Continuing down and across the next draw, I reached a narrow strip of timber and worked my way out through the thigh-deep snow to look over the edge.

I couldn't fully see the steep, upper end of the draw, so I moved farther out onto the point for a better view. When I turned to look back, I spotted the big bull rising from his bed. Realizing the elk was only a few steps from going over the timbered ridge, I turned and got off a quick, offhand shot at 200 yards. It was a clean miss and my heart was pounding as I chambered another round.

The Grand Slam bullet from the second shot slammed home, but the big bull never broke his stride. My third shot broke him down, however, and I watched as he slid for 300 yards down the steep snow-covered draw.

As I approached the downed bull, my thoughts were racing. How big was he? Was he the 6x6 bull I'd dreamed about for years? The closer I got, the more I began to think maybe this was the quality of bull that had always evaded me. I counted six big points on one side and seven on the other with long sweeping main beams. What a bull!

It took Neil and I until 8:30 the following night to pack out my elk, but we both agreed, the tougher they are to get out, the longer you remember the hunt. It was a great adventure and I am absolutely thrilled with my big Montana bull that gross-scored 378 4/8 with a final net score of 361 4/8 B&C.

It was a tough but successful Montana hunt for Mike Russell.

ONE INCREDIBLE YEAR

BY JOE DANCA

As a new subscriber to your magazine I want to let you know how much I enjoy it. As I read about the experiences of your members, I thought you might want to hear about the incredible year of elk hunting I had a few years back.

It all started in July when I opened an envelope from the Montana Fish and Game Department that contained one of the few nonresident permits for the late hunt near Gardiner. The chance to hunt the big bulls of Yellowstone after they leave the Park is truly a once-in-a-lifetime opportunity.

February found me hunting with Gardiner native, Dan McDonald, on the Royal Teton Ranch that borders Yellowstone Park. After strug-

Only two nonresident tags were offered in the area where Joe took his Utah bull.

gling for a couple of days with the steep terrain and thigh-deep snow, we were able to make a good stalk and harvest a beautiful 325-class 6x6 bull. In my mind, the hunt-of-a-lifetime ended with the harvesting of the bull-of-a-lifetime.

Incredibly, July of the following year again found me opening an envelope with another once-in-a-lifetime tag inside, this time for the state of Utah. My friend Craig Purse and I applied for the most difficult-to-draw limited-entry hunt in the state with the idea of accumulating bonus points. With only two nonresident tags given each year, the odds of our party application being successful on our first year of applying were almost nonexistent. So much for the odds.

Craig and I agreed we would need as much help as we could get to hunt our area. After thoroughly checking out our options, we used the services of Alan Yardley and Mike White from Beaver, Utah.

Late September found us in southwest Utah, only seven short months after my Gardiner hunt. After a successful and exciting opening morning hunt, I attached my tag to an enormous 6x7. He had 52-inch main beams and grossed 385 B&C. The bull-of-a-lifetime, so far.

The incredible year began with the harvesting of this 325 B&C Montana bull.

Joe's 385 B&C Utah bull has 52-inch main beams.

NEVADA

Jim and Patty Hatcher pose with Jim's Nevada nontypical.

The bull's antler characteristics were consistent during his last four years.

NONTYPICAL NEVADA BULL

Jim Hatcher, an avid elk hunter from Bend, Oregon, purchased a Nevada Governor's elk tag from the Rocky Mountain Elk Foundation. This permit allowed Jim to hunt with rifle during the September rut.

While researching his area Jim became acquainted with the Marques brothers, who live near the unit that is located just outside Ely, Nevada. These four brothers live for elk, spending as much time as possible with them at all times of the year. The Marques have even gone so far as to name every bull in the area.

The brothers had watched this bull for a number of years and collected his sheds for the last three. Amazingly, one of them had guessed the bull's score to within three inches. They had also spotted a bull in this area they estimated would gross over 400 B&C.

Jim's bull was living with a number of cows near a large sagebrush flat. The bull's preoccupation with his harem allowed Jim to make a difficult stalk through the low cover. A Winchester .300 magnum loaded with 180-grain Nosler Partition bullets was used to harvest his bull.

The nontypical score on Jim's 12 year-old Nevada trophy is 379 B&C. After field dressing and removing the head and neck, the bull still weighed 550 pounds.

Bob and Ray with Bob's 340 B&C Nevada bull.

AN AWFUL BULL

BY BOB WELLS

After nearly two decades of religious applying, I finally drew a coveted Nevada bull elk tag. I'll never forget the thrill I experienced as I pulled that envelope from the mailbox. Almost afraid to know, I tilted it toward the sky in hopes of a sneak preview of the results. My hands started to shake as I read "Bull Elk, Area 162." Jumping up and down I ran over to my work crew yelling, "I got it, I got it!" That was just the beginning of the longest high I've ever had; in fact, I still have it.

After painstaking research, I finally chose Timberline Outfitters, Nick Perchetti and Pard Galvin, Box 65 Tonopah, NV 89049, (702) 482-3361 or 482-6422. I dug deep trying to unearth something bad about these guys but came up empty.

Eager to to see my area, I booked a late-August pack trip with Nick and Pard for my girlfriend and I. They packed us in to the same camp where I would be hunting in September. We saw a large herd of elk that included 16 bulls. My fire was really getting stoked now! The three weeks that remained before my hunt were the longest I've ever experienced.

My brother, Ray, traveled down from Montana to join me on this hunt-of-a-lifetime. The day before our adventure was to begin, we drove to an abandoned ranch near the trailhead. That night, we soaked under the stars in a cattle tank fed by a natural hot spring.

Early the next morning, we were off to meet up with Nick and Pard. After an uneventful trip into camp, everyone stayed busy organizing their tents, hoping to make the time go by more quickly.

I can't say I slept like a rock that night. Let's just say I was sure glad when 4:00 a.m. arrived. We all enjoyed a good breakfast, saddled up and headed up the mountain in the dark. Reaching the top at first light, Nick immediately spotted a bull. Quickly, we jumped off our horses and tied them to some nearby trees. The bull was 300 yards away when Nick spotted him, but he walked to within 75 yards of us after he mistook our horses for cow elk. He was a beautiful 6-point with an extra 15-inch tine sticking straight out from the left main beam. I thought Ray was going to die when I decided to pass. It was just to early in the hunt—I didn't

95

Nick and Bob packing the bull out of Nevada's Unit 162.

want it to be over that soon. As we watched, three more bulls, including a good 6-point, joined the 7x6. We saw a total of 11 bulls on the first day of my hunt.

At camp that evening we learned Pard's group had taken a huge 5-point. We all shook hands and slapped backs for a while, then headed to bed in anticipation of another glorious day of elk hunting.

The plan for the second day was to hunt our way over to Pard's elk where we would help him load it on the mules and then hunt back toward camp. Just before we reached the dead elk, we spotted a huge 6-point bugling from a hillside 400 yards away. What a sight and sound! I thought another hunter we had seen was making a sneak on the big bull so I never got off my horse. As it turned out he didn't even see the bull. We never did catch up to that monster, but we sure had fun trying.

After reaching Pard's bull around noon, we ate our lunches and began glassing. An hour later Ray spotted a cow near a stand of mahogany about a mile away. Soon, a 5-point was chased out of the trees by an unseen herd bull. During the next 30 minutes we saw several other bulls and cows. That's when "he" made his brief but fatal appearance. When I saw the big bull through a small opening in the mahogany, I knew immediately he had to be mine.

An hour's ride took us to the base of the hill where we had seen the big bull. We tied up the horses and climbed to a rock outcropping just below the mahogany patch. Two cows that were bedded 50 yards away suddenly caught our scent. Now it was show time. As I rose to my feet, the crotch of a tree made a perfect rest for my rifle. Several cows and bulls ran out of the timber, then Nick yelled, "There he is, shoot him!"

Three quick shots put the bull down for good. When we walked up to that monster, I couldn't believe my eyes. As Nick would say, "He was an awful bull." Everyone pitched in to help care for my elk and we had the antlers back to camp by 9:00 p.m.

Nick had field judged the big 5-point at 345 B&C. The bull was officially scored later at 340 6/8 B&C, not a bad guess, Nick! The hunt of-a-lifetime came off without a hitch and Ray and I share a memory that will last forever.

Dan Cominsky with his 356 B&C bull.

MATCHING BULLS

BY MIKE ROSS

Nevada's first Rocky Mountain elk transplant from Yellowstone Park into the rugged Schell Creek Range of White Pine County took place in the 1930s. Since then, the state has continually expanded the range of these magnificent animals until now they inhabit at least six mountain ranges.

In 1979, 49 elk were transplanted to Table Mountain in the Monitor Mountains of central Nevada. The first hunt took place five years later in 1984.

A Table Mountain hunt in 1995 produced an almost matched pair of big bulls scoring 356 and 356 4/8 B&C.

The first hunter, Joe Freshman of Reno, hired the services of Jim and Karen Stahl, owners of Mustang Outfitters, P.O. Box 1149, Round Mountain, NV 89045, Ph. (702) 964-2145, for his precious opportunity to score on a trophy wapiti. Three days were spent bugling in big bulls and video-taping them in the beautiful aspen parks of Table Mountain. A super bull was finally spotted at a distance of 400 yards by Joe and his party. As the bull dropped into one of the many rocky gorges thick with mountain mahogany, Joe connected with three fatal shots.

Even after packing the 460 pounds of meat 10 miles out to the trail-head, Joe was all grins with his beautiful bull that grossed 379 1/8 and netted 356 4/8 B&C.

The second hunter, Dan Cominsky of Stateline, Nevada, booked his elk hunt with another central Nevada guide service, Big Smoky Valley Outfitters, HCR 60 Box 77206, Round Mountain, Nevada 89045-9801, Ph. (702) 964-1207. Outfitters Bill and Donna Berg are both longtime residents and hunters of the high mountains of central Nevada.

Over 30 miles were ridden in two days as the party hunted the high country of Table Mountain. Several mediocre bulls were bugled in, but nothing Dan was interested in.

The hunters awoke at 4:30 a.m. on day three to find their elk bugle soaking wet in one of the saddle bags. As Bill Berg blew on the bugle, making all sorts of wet sputtering sounds, a bull answered back from right above camp. Not wanting to scare off the elk, Bill stopped bugling and saddled the horses. The bull, however, continued to bugle and move closer to camp. A quick decision was made to leave the horses and go after the bull on foot.

Blowing the wet bugle occasionally, Dan and his party made their way up the hillside in the early morning light. Suddenly, they found themselves within 25 feet of the monster bull. The big rack, which was all they could see above the rocks, suddenly spun around as the elk winded the hunters. Dan steadied himself on a rock as the bull went crashing through the trees, and just as it broke into an opening, he fired.

As the bull charged on down the canyon, Dan thought he missed his second shot, but Donna swore she heard the great "whump" sound of a solid hit. Bill picked up the bull's track and the hunters followed it down into a rocky, mountain mahogany draw where Dan's prized trophy was found. Another fine 356 B&C bull had hit the dust on beautiful aspen-carpeted Table Mountain, thus completing a matched pair of bulls.

At 356 4/8 B&C, Joe Freshman's bull is almost identical to Dan's.

NOW I BELIEVE IN MIRACLES

BY DON J. DEES

After several unsuccessful years of trying for a coveted bull elk rifle tag in Nevada, I applied for an archery bull tag and drew out. I have hunted all my life, but until last year had never chased elk. In fact, I had never even seen an elk in the wild. From the information I received from fellow hunters, I knew this would be the hunt-of-a-lifetime.

I was quick to enlist the help of Joel Blakeslee, a good friend who had spent a lot of time trapping in my area. Since he also mapped all the vegetation in the Ely area for the Forest Service, it is safe to say Joel knows the area as well as, or better than, anyone.

Two days before the September 9 opener, we awoke to the sound of bulls bugling all around us. Joel and I decided to concentrate our search in an area where we had spotted at least 10 mature bulls.

Opening morning I tried hunting from a water hole blind. However with over 200 inches of precipitation the previous winter, the elk were not watering in any one place consistently. Fortunately, after three months of practice I was able to bugle fairly well. It looked as if that was the only way I was going to get a bull.

The second morning, I bugled a 6-point bull across a large grass field to within 35 yards. Though I guessed he would score around 320, I decided to pass, hoping to find something bigger. Over the course of the week I had cause to regret this decision more than once.

Joel and I decided to move camp and try some different areas. Six days into the hunt we finally located an elk we thought was the granddaddy of all bulls. Because of his enormous size and deep rumbling bugle, we named the bull T-Rex. Joel estimated this old boy would score over 400 P&Y.

For four days and nights we climbed to the top of the plateau where T-Rex, his 30-cow harem, and a half dozen satellite bulls lived. Unfortunately, the swirling Nevada winds prevented me from getting any closer than 50 yards to Rex. Even then, he winded me before I could get a clear shot.

Rex had beaten us and I did not have the energy to chase him anymore. The next day I put Joel on a plane to Reno so that he could get back to work. That night, I rented a room in Ely to regroup and catch up on my sleep.

In desperation I called an old friend of Joel's for some advice. Chuck Marques and his brothers have guided the recipient of the Governor's elk in Nevada tag for many years. These guys know just about every big bull in the area and have most of them on film. Chuck offered to spend a day showing me some of his more productive spots. We got into several good bulls, but a shooting opportunity never arrived.

I decided to return to the place where Joel and I had spent the first two days of my hunt. For some reason, I had a really good feeling about that spot.

Arriving at Mt. Grafton, I parked the truck and used my quad to drive in the rest of the way to our old campsite. I had no sooner shut off the engine when I heard a bugle from the pinion-junipers 100 yards away.

Throwing on my backpack, I put on a face mask and headed up the hill in pursuit of the as yet unseen bull. Bugling as I walked, I could hear the bull less than 50 yards ahead. I stopped at the edge of a baseball diamond-sized clearing to see if I could bugle him in. If he was a 6-point, I would take the shot.

After five minutes of bugling, cow calling and tree raking, I spotted a large set of antlers coming slowly through the trees toward me. I counted six beautiful points as I came to full draw. Just as he was about to clear the last juniper, he stopped with only part of his nose and rack in view. He stood dead still for what seemed like an eternity until finally, I couldn't hold at full draw. In a final effort, I kicked the tree I was hiding behind. That disturbance was just enough to make him rush into the open at 35 yards. I quickly drew, aimed and let her fly.

The way the bull bolted, I first thought I had missed. However, when I got to where he had been standing, there was my bloodied shaft with the broadhead broken off. It was then I noticed the incredible blood trail. After an hour-long wait and 300 yards of tracking, I found my bull. He was no T-Rex, but he was all I could ever ask for. My bull grossed 341 1/8 and netted 330 P&Y.

During my 14 days in the mountains around Ely, Nevada, I saw over 70 bulls, 30 of which were 6-point or better. Not a day goes by that I don't think of this hunt-of-a-lifetime.

Don bugled his bull in for the 35-yard shot.

Bill, left, and his father, with Bill's 366 2/8 B&C bull.

THANKSGIVING DAY BULL

BY BILL BALSI JR.

My dad and I arrived in Ely, Nevada on November 14 for three days of elk scouting with Chuck and David Marques. We saw several trophy class bulls and I was anxious for the season to begin.

On opening day, David Marques, Mark Mannens, Dad and I hunted an area where David had seen a 360-plus bull the evening before. We saw a total of seven bulls, including one big 6x6. Unfortunately, he was running through the trees and I was unable to get a shot.

Over the next two days we saw several bulls in the 300 to 340 B&C class. The 340 bull was tempting but we decided to keep looking for the big bull we had seen on opening day. A 360 B&C, 7x6 was located late on the third day but it got dark before we could complete our stalk.

On the fourth day of my hunt we spotted a big 6x9 but couldn't get on him. We also saw many smaller bulls but nothing I was interested in.

Day five was very exciting! We found "Felix," a big 7x7, 365 B&C bull. Murph and David Marques and I attempted a stalk and got within 500 yards of that great bull, but he just wouldn't step out of the trees. I had one of his hind quarters in my crosshairs for over 10 minutes before he finally slipped into the timber. We tried pushing Felix out of a thick stand of trees, but when he appeared he was over 400 yards away at a full run. All I could see was a flash of his antlers every so often as he made his escape.

Chuck, Trevor and Jim Marques met my father and me at 2:30 on Thanksgiving morning. I spotted a big bull over a mile away at 6:30 a.m., and as it got light we could tell he was worthy of a closer look. Chuck and I took off at full speed to a ridge top directly across from the bull. He was still feeding as we studied him through our spotting scopes and determined he was the quality of bull I had been looking for.

Because there wasn't time to move closer before the bull moved into the trees to bed down, I was forced to shoot from the top of the ridge. It was a case of now or never as I steadied my 7mm Sako topped with a Leupold 3x10 scope. I positioned the crosshairs just over the top of the elk's back as he stood broadside looking in my direction. Chuck, Dad,

Trevor and Jim were all watching through their spotting scopes as the shot rang out.

The bull wheeled and came straight downhill plowing into a dead six-inch tree. Bark and tree limbs flew in all directions, then everything was quiet. When the bull stepped from the trees into a small clearing a few seconds later, I hit him with another shot. Then, as he turned and headed toward the heavy timber, I fired again, putting him down for good.

The closer I got to the fallen bull, the larger he looked. His main beams were 57 1/2 inches long and he grossed 372 with a net score of 366 2/8 B&C. After the rest of our party caught up to us with the pickups, we called Ely where the remaining Marques brothers and Bill Adair graciously agreed to forgo their Thanksgiving dinners to help us with the packing. By the time we took pictures, quartered the bull, and packed him out, it was three o'clock in the afternoon.

Over 40 bulls were located on my hunt, including five that would score over 350 B&C. I would like to thank the Marques brothers; Chuck, Murph, David and Jim, who helped on the hunt. My thanks also to Bill Adair, who helped pack out and video my bull; my good friend, Mark Mannens, and most of all Dad, who is always there for me.

NEW MEXICO

Jeff's bull officially scored 336 6/8 P&Y.

New Mexico Archery Bull

By Jeff Lampe

On opening morning of bow season, my hunting partner, Glenn Vlass, and I were in the back-country of northern New Mexico. We had previously scouted the area and found it to hold a large number of mature bulls.

The first few days produced several nice bulls, but we didn't have the opportunity for a shot. Glenn and I were both holding out for a respectable bull, but hunting was difficult due to hot temperatures and a full moon. The elk were leaving the openings after first light and did not return until almost dark.

Mid-week found us backpacking into a new area that we knew held quite a few nice bulls. Shortly after arriving, we started seeing elk. That evening, two small herds fed into a meadow across the valley. Each group included a large herd bull caked with mud from wallowing.

As we split up to hunt different parts of the valley, bulls were bugling all around. Glenn watched three different 6-points use the same wallow but was unable to get close enough for a shot. I was able to get within range of a good bull but darkness forced me to back off.

The next morning we were back in the same area at first light. The elk, however, were held up in the trees so we decided to wait until evening.

By late afternoon, we were set up on two heavily used wallows. Shortly after I arrived at my position, I heard the first bugle. An hour later, several cows were standing on the far side of the meadow, looking in my direction.

Suddenly, a large, heavy-horned bull appeared behind the cows and pushed them toward the wallow. Before I knew it, the cows were watering off to my left, just out of sight. The big bull was watering in front of me at 20 yards. After drinking, he stepped into the wallow and turned broadside.

A bugle from up the valley caught his attention and he bugled back.

As several more elk entered the meadow, he looked in their direction. In one fluid motion, I rose to my knees and came to full draw. My clicker went off and the arrow was gone, its yellow fletching disappearing behind the bull's front shoulder.

When the bull ran from the wallow, I saw the arrow fall from his opposite side. As he tried to run back across the meadow, he stopped, stood motionless for several seconds, and then crashed to the ground 50 yards from the wallow.

*(**Notes:** Jeff, who lives in Loveland, Colorado, shoots a Custom Bighorn recurve. He uses cedar shafts with Grizzly broadheads. At one time, Jeff suffered from "target panic." He recommends a device called the Clickery-Klick to help overcome this problem. The clicker forces you to achieve the same draw length on every shot.)*

My Hard Luck Bull

By Frank Marczak

Elk hunting is supposed to be hard, but this was ridiculous. My legs were weary, and my lungs were on fire. If I had been tracking a bull or a big mulie it would have been okay, but I was trying to get back to the cabin after my truck had broken down.

I was hunting on a 22,000-acre private ranch in an area of New Mexico known for big bulls. A friend, Chris Curren, accompanied me on this hunt as an observer. He was getting a crash course in big game hunting.

One day earlier, I spotted a 4x4 bull feeding in a clearing. I raised my rifle and fired offhand as he entered the timber. My shot went wide and, lo and behold, there was blood running from my nose. When I shouldered my rifle I was off balance, you can pop yourself pretty good with a .338!

Juan, the owner of the ranch, had agreed to guide me if I needed the help. When I came off the mountain, I found him cutting wood in one of his pastures. I figured the sooner he was through, the sooner we would hunt, so I pitched in and within a few hours we were on our way.

After reaching our destination, we parked the truck and continued on foot. We paralleled a ridge for several hundred yards until we broke out onto a knoll overlooking a sagebrush-covered opening. There couldn't be a more likely spot.

Within 20 minutes we saw several cows and two small bulls working their way down through the trees into the sage directly in front of us. Juan commented there had to be a big bull back in the trees.

Farther down, another herd of elk appeared at the edge of the sage. This bunch had a big-bodied 3x3 with them. It was nearly dark and I figured my time had run out. Leaning on a dead pinion snag, I put the crosshairs on the 3x3's neck. I was just about to squeeze the trigger when Juan slapped my back and whispered, "The herd bull! Shoot the herd bull!"

As I worked my way around the deadfall I was using for a rest, my eyes bugged out! Entering the sage flat were 30 cows followed by four or five bulls.

Dropping to my knees, I set my scope on the largest bull and pulled the trigger. As I ejected the round, Murphy's Law kicked in. My bolt wouldn't feed the remaining shells.

We solved the problem by dropping the floor plate on my rifle and emptying the magazine. Now all I had to do was grasp for the loose shells in the dust at my feet. I always wanted a single shot rifle, now I had one!

The elk were now heading back into the safety of the timber. I zeroed in on an opening, and when the big bull passed, I squeezed the trigger. I told Juan I was sure my second shot was a solid hit, but I could see he was disappointed.

I felt something hot running down my face. Again I had hugged my scope too close, so now I had two more crescents on my forehead to add to the one on my nose.

As Juan left for the truck, I shouldered my rifle and, swabbing the blood from my face, headed toward the sage flat. Cursing myself at the blown once-in-a-lifetime opportunity, I thought about the long ride back home. There was one day left to hunt, but after this…would I want to?

The harvest moon was in full glow and there was no need for a flashlight. Slowly, I worked my way through the waist-high sage, my eyes scanning the area ahead.

Suddenly, towering over the sagebrush, I saw four points and a main beam! When I approached the bull, he had yet to expire. Saying a prayer for the two of us, I placed a shot into the base of his neck.

Juan drove up, smiling from ear to ear. I let out a carnal yell, and we slapped each other on the back. Moving the bull for some pictures took all the strength we had left. I found two bruised cigars in my backpack. I quit smoking 10 years ago, but that day I had a feeling, I also had a match.

As we stared at this magnificent animal we figured out the puzzle. My first shot had missed, but the second had not. The 250-grain Nosler bullet had broken the bull's back, passed through a lung, and ended up between two ribs under the skin.

The next day we delivered my bull to Wilderness Taxidermy in Chama where he unofficially scored 347 B&C gross. He was a 7x7 with heavy 52-inch main beams.

This was my first bull in four years of hunting elk. I have taken my share of game, but no other hunt compared to this. Even with all the hard luck Chris and I endured, I would do it all over in spades. As for my bloody nose and forehead, you could hit me with a shovel if all my elk hunts ended like this.

Frank Marczak and his big New Mexico bull.

With eight inches broken off the left royal, Terry's bull still scores 343 1/8 LHS.

LAST MINUTE BULL

BY TERRY MASON

New Mexico's muzzleloader elk season was down to its last day and still I didn't have the monster bull I so badly wanted. Huge bulls had been seen and missed during the archery season in this area, so it was just a matter of finding them. My guide, Jude Gabaldon, and I saw several bulls and cows that morning but nothing I was interested in putting my tag on. Now it was down to the last evening. We decided to hunt an area where we had seen three good bulls come out to feed two days before. From there, we could also watch the mountain where one of the other hunters in camp had missed a 400-point bull.

As the sun began to set, we moved farther up the mountain so we would be close enough for a stalk should a bull present itself. The glassing was easier with the sun behind the mountain and soon Jude said, "I see a good bull, maybe a 340." We scrambled to get closer.

I had hoped to shoot a 380-class bull, but when I saw this one he looked good, with long beams and a wide spread. The bull was feeding down a dry creek bed through the oak brush in our direction. As we moved closer in the gathering darkness, Jude said almost prophetically, "You're going to kill this bull."

The wait was exciting. From our vantage point 160 yards above a small clearing, we could hear the elk walking through the leaves. I had good confidence in my .50-caliber White Systems Model 91 that was sighted in for 130 yards. However, I knew at this steep angle I would have to aim a little low so as not to shoot over him.

In a kneeling position I waited, hoping he would step into the clearing before it got too dark to accurately place the shot. With only minutes of shooting light remaining, he suddenly moved into the open. At the shot he spun, ran a couple of steps downhill, and dropped. I quickly reloaded but in the brush couldn't see him well enough to get off another shot.

We hurried down to find he had died in a very awkward position with his brow tines wedged around a tree and his body flipped downhill through the antlers. Unable to move the bull, we struggled to field dress him by flashlight.

Returning with more help the next morning, we skinned the bull and discovered my Accuracy Unlimited 450-grain Copper Head bullet had completely penetrated the chest.

Even with eight inches broken off the left royal point, my 6x6 managed to gross 343 1/8 B&C, LHS. The main beams measure 54 inches and the rack has an inside spread of 45 inches. I was thrilled to get such a nice trophy for my first muzzleloader elk…I am definitely going back. Next time I will hold out for an even bigger bull, but hopefully I won't have to wait until the last minute of the last day.

THE PRINCE OF WHITEWATER

BY ROGER BAILEY

The long shadows disappeared and it began to get cold as the sun slowly went down. With the temperature rising to 70 degrees earlier in the day, I had neglected to bring my jacket. The 40-degree evening temperature made me sorry I'd forgotten it.

Greg Gurr, Mike Rosenlof and I had arrived in Socorro County, New Mexico six days earlier. We were now three days into the five-day special muzzleloader elk hunt for which we had drawn tags. A couple of

Roger, with partners Greg Gurr and Mike Rosenlof.

117

good bulls had been located before the hunt started, but they had disappeared with the arrival of other hunters to the area.

Opening day of the musket hunt found me near a water tank I had discovered two days earlier. It looked like a great location, but all that showed up were turkeys, deer, and a couple of coyotes. Mike and Greg spent the day in other locations but they too finished the day empty-handed. Elk hunting in Unit 17 was beginning to look real grim.

My hunting partners and I went to the bottom of Sergeant Canyon on Monday morning. A road ran clear to the top, but we parked our truck, preferring to walk. Nobody in their right mind would drive right through the middle of the prime elk country they were planning to hunt. When we reached the top, there were four trucks and two ATVs already there. We had seen a 4-point bull and a couple of cows, but there were more hunters than elk.

We decided to split up again, with Mike and Greg going to Bitter Canyon while I headed for East Whitewater Canyon. Shortly after noon, three cows and a 4-point bull came rumbling out of the trees right into the water tank I was watching. With only two days left to hunt I was very tempted to fill my tag, but I didn't drive 750 miles to take a smaller bull than those I'd seen before the hunt started.

As the hours passed, my thoughts turned to my 14 year-old son, Brandon, who was on his first mule deer hunt back home in Utah. Though I wished I could be with him, I knew he was in good hands with my cousin, Brent.

Chilled by the falling temperatures, I left my blind and started the 1 1/2 mile journey to the truck. On my way back, I noticed movement on one of the ridges. Through my binoculars I could see about 10 head of elk, including one large bull. The 20 minutes of daylight remaining wouldn't give me time to reach the elk, so I just watched them and studied the area until dark. As I walked on through the darkness, I decided "The Prince of Whitewater" would be a fitting name for the big bull.

When I got back to camp, I asked Mike and Greg what their plans were for the next day's hunt. They hadn't seen anything worth shooting, so they agreed to go with me back to East Whitewater.

The next morning, Mike and Greg went high while I stayed low. If we were lucky, we could keep the elk between us. The going was slow. With no rain in over a month it was very dry and noisy.

Mike jumped the bull, but it was too quick for him to get a shot. I heard the racket long before I saw the elk coming toward me. Suddenly, there was the bull! I picked an open spot where he would pass and raised the Thompson Renegade. As the bull cleared the trees, he caught either my scent or movement and immediately quartered away. As he

118

Roger's New Mexico bull net scores 357 6/8 LHS.

passed through my peep sight I pulled the trigger. For a moment, all I could see was smoke.

Bull fever had set in and I wasn't having much luck frantically trying to reload my rifle. Just as I was ramming another 545-grain Buck Buster Slug down the barrel, I heard Mike start yelling. I ran around a small knoll and there lay my bull. The Prince had traveled only 35 yards before going down.

What a magnificent animal! His large 6x6 frame had 11 1/2-inch bases, a 46 1/2-inch inside spread and 54-inch main beams. With only 3 4/8 inches of deductions, he officially scored 361 2/8 gross and netted 357 6/8 B&C, LHS.

On the way home I called Brandon on Mike's cellular phone. He told me he had shot a nice 2-point buck at almost the exact time I shot my bull. The 13-hour drive back home was not going to be so long now.

U T A H

Gary and son Nathan pose with Gary's Utah bull.

Utah Trophy Bull

By Gary Larsen

My son, Nathan, and I thoroughly enjoy reading *The Eastmans' Journal*. Like others in your publication, we have become firm believers in applying for limited-entry tags to gain access to quality hunting units and trophy animals.

The luck of the draw fell my way when I drew a limited-entry bull elk tag in western Utah. After pre-scouting for five days and locating several mature bulls, I was eager to return for the rifle hunt during the rut.

On opening morning, we were the only hunters in our area. Accompanied by Nathan, my brother, Steve, and his two boys, we proceeded to check out some of the bulls we had seen while scouting.

After passing on a nice 6x6 satellite bull in the morning, a rain-delayed afternoon hunt found us in the middle of a power play among four bugling, tree-thrashing bulls. As each mature bull bellowed a challenge, a competitor would interrupt. This enraged each participant enough to answer even more vigorously as cows and immature bulls scattered in all directions through the thick cedars.

We were able to stalk to within 70 yards of one of the bulls before he started to move off. The bugling 6x6 bull led us over a mile through the cedars before he presented an open target. A single 180-grain, 30-06 bullet put the rutting bull down for good.

The bull's first three points on either side average over 18 inches long. The symmetrical 6x6 scores an unofficial 332 7/8 B&C gross.

Jerry Leavitt with his first elk, a fine Utah 6x5.

Ron, left, and Glendon Anderson pose with their father's huge Utah bull.

RECORD BOOK UTAH BULL

BY JIM LEAVITT

My sons, Jerry and Josh, and I are fascinated with bull elk. We would hunt, photograph or look for sheds full time if we could. As we read the elk hunting stories in *The Journal*, we feel a little bad that we don't live in Arizona, Colorado, Wyoming or Nevada, all states with huge elk.

We have taken two nice bulls in Colorado that scored between 250 and 300 B&C. Since we haven't been able to draw for a trophy elk unit in Utah, we have taken only smaller bulls from the open units. In fact, we have taken up shed antler hunting as our best chance to collect trophy-size antlers. We have found several sets that score from 330 to 360 B&C.

You can imagine our excitement in locating a true Boone and Crockett bull that was taken in Salina Canyon, only 25 miles from our home in Annabella, Utah.

One of our friends, while looking at our largest shed antlers, said, "My dad has a set mounted that he shot back in 1972 that is much bigger than these."

We thought, "That's impossible. Not in Utah!"

A few days later, we rough-scored the Anderson bull at 386 gross, with a net score of 380 B&C. Sure enough, this was huge for Utah.

*(**Notes:** The following account was relayed by Glendon Anderson who accompanied his father, Miles, on the hunt for this record book Utah bull.)*

At the time my father took this bull, several people told us the big rack would probably make the Boone and Crockett Record Book. However, the antlers hung in my father's house for over 20 years before we finally had the bull measured. Boone and Crockett scorer, Dennis Shirley, officially scored the head at 381 5/8 B&C net, which places him in the top three ever taken in Utah.

This bull was harvested in an area our family has hunted for many years. I know there were more big bulls then than there are now. In fact, my cousin took a huge nontypical on the same day my father harvested his bull. Though there are more elk now, there just isn't the quality of bulls.

Dad's bull was taken on a September hunt, right in the middle of the rut. Everyone had left camp early in the morning, long before we rode out at 10:30. The other hunters went right past the herd of elk that held the big bull.

We rode into the middle of the herd with our horses and Dad fired twice at the bull with his old .303 British Enfield. The huge bull turned and disappeared with the rest of the herd.

Anticipating the direction the elk were taking, we tried to cut them off, but they slipped past us in the timber.

As we continued our hunt, I told my father I thought he'd hit the bull, and I was going back to look for him. He told me to go ahead, but he was pretty sure he had missed.

I jumped the bull not 20 yards from where Dad had shot. As I approached the wounded elk, it jumped to its feet and ran into a thicket. Eventually we found the bull again, and were able to finish him.

While we were dressing the elk, Lee Robertson from the Utah Division of Wildlife came by and filmed us for a television station. We tried later to retrieve the video, but it had been thrown away.

Data On Bull:

	Right Antler	Left Antler
Number of points	6	6
Length of main beam	58 in.	57 6/8 in.
Length first point	15 1/8 in.	14 7/8 in.
Length second point	14 3/8 in.	15 7/8 in.
Length third point	17 3/8 in.	17 3/8 in.
Length royal points	21 2/8 in	18 3/8 in.
Length sixth point	16 5/8 in.	16 5/8 in.
Circumference of base	9 in.	9 in.

BEGINNER'S LUCK

BY DENNIS B. CROPPER

My son, Wesley, took this bull from a limited draw area in Utah. It was only the second year he had applied for a limited hunt. Of course, after years of applying I had to take the ribbing for not drawing out again.

In preparation for the hunt, we came up with some hot loads for Wesley's model 70 Winchester 30-06. Our choice of bullets was 165-grain Noslers. I knew they could do the job.

We purchased all the needed topographic maps and talked to Fish and Game people, ranchers and hunters to find out all we could about the area. When we had time, Wesley and I visited the area to scout for elk. The homework, along with beginner's luck, paid off.

Opening morning, just at daylight, the bull began to bugle. We followed the sound for about a mile before getting a glimpse of him. The conditions were perfect as we stalked to within 125 yards.

I quietly reminded Wes where he should hold for a clean kill. He is only 16 and I knew he needed to keep his mind on the point-of-aim instead of the huge rack. The first shot was right on target, but the bull didn't go down. I told Wesley to fire again as the bull trotted away. The second shot was also well placed, but still the old veteran refused to fall. As Wesley prepared to fire a third time, the bull dropped.

I don't know who was more excited, my son or me. Wesley and I shared the thrill of a great trophy hunt and I am very proud of him.

I really enjoy reading *The Journal* and seeing the great trophy animals others have taken. Keep up the good work!

Mack's Utah bull green scored 367 B&C.

MACK'S BEAST

BY CHARLES CROWLEY

Having enjoyed my subscription to *The Journal* for over a year, I would like to thank the crew at *Eastmans'* for their contribution to big game hunters. The information found in *The Journal* is a big help to those of us who don't have a lot of time to do our own research.

Over the years, I have seen many good bull elk while hunting mule deer in eastern Utah. Last year we sent in our elk applications and, though I didn't draw, a friend of mine, Mack Galbreath, was lucky enough to receive a permit. Since Mack was unfamiliar with the area, I agreed to accompany him on his hunt. Neither of us had hunted elk before so we looked forward to an exciting trip.

We trailered our riding horses from Fresno, California to Utah in mid-September. Arrangements were made with a local mule packer to haul our gear to the campsite located about 4 1/2 hours from the end of the road.

Hoping to spend some time learning about elk, we set up camp 1 1/2 days before season opened. We knew it was a sign of good things to come when a bull bugled as we were unpacking the mules.

After quickly setting up camp, we hiked up the ridge toward the sound of the bugle. Hunting elk during the rut proved to be a great advantage as the sound of the bulls' bugling allowed us to easily locate them. We hadn't gone far before we spotted the bull that we heard from camp. Though its antlers were fairly heavy, with decent tine length, we knew there were even better bulls in the area.

The next day we located several bulls and, unbelievably, all but one were 6x6s. That evening, however, we spotted a monster bull that dwarfed all the others—a real "Beast"! As Mack viewed the bull from across a canyon, he knew it was the kind of trophy he had always dreamed of. With the season set to open the following morning, we left the old boy undisturbed and returned to camp.

Rising at 3:30 the next morning, we headed for the ridge where we'd seen the bull the night before. The morning's hunt proved unproductive, so we decided to move across the canyon. We had no sooner arrived at our new location, than we spotted an exceptionally wide 6x7 at about 1,200 yards.

As we studied the 6x7, a bugle suddenly broke the silence about a half mile down the ridge from where we'd seen the Beast the night before. Hoping to increase our chances of finding the bull, we split up and headed in different directions. I hadn't gone far before I spotted an elk through my spotting scope and, with one quick look, I knew it was Mack's bull!

Running full speed up the ridge, I found my buddy and told him what I'd seen. We hurried back to the flat and found the bull and his three cows still feeding contentedly. As the elk wandered in and out of the timber, Mack took one look and exclaimed, "That's him!"

Mack was carrying a pair of Leica binoculars that, with their built-in digital range finder, are truly an incredible instrument. Using the range finder, we determined the bull to be at a distance of 850 meters, which is over 900 yards.

Long-distance shots such as Mack faced are the reason he carries a custom-made 30-378 rifle. The cartridge is a .378 Weatherby necked down to .30 caliber. Mack's special handload pushes a 220-grain bullet at 3225 fps. His scope has dots built into it that show where to hold for distances from 300 to 1000 meters.

That gun is designed to kill an elk at 1000 meters so I told Mack, "Shoot him!" He looked at me like I was crazy and replied, "Let's try to get closer."

We dropped out of sight behind a ridge and hurried in the bull's direction. The elk were feeding in fairly heavy timber, so finding an opening through which to get a clear shot was difficult.

Moving closer, we finally found a shooting lane complete with a fallen log for Mack to use as a rest. Mack handed me the binoculars as he moved into position behind the log. Through the range finder we determined the bull was now at 637 meters or 700 yards. I was starting to get nervous when I whispered to Mack, "Hurry, everything is perfect, he's just standing there—shoot!" Not getting a response, I turned to find my partner calmly stuffing toilet paper into his ears. Mack is afflicted with constant ringing in his ears and he didn't want to aggravate his condition by shooting without ear protection. Talk about staying calm under pressure!

Once the ear plugs were in place, Mack rested his rifle across the log and touched it off. The bull turned and stumbled downhill for 50 yards before going down for good.

The excitement of our success was almost overwhelming as I slapped Mack on the back and congratulated him. With darkness fast approaching, we hurriedly packed our gear and headed toward the elk. When we reached the area where the bull had fallen, everything looked different than it had from across the canyon. Difficulty in finding your downed game is one drawback of extreme long-distance shooting.

When we found the bull 1 1/2 hours later, he truly was a beast! The 6x6 antlers green-scored 367 B&C, and were very heavy with good, long tines. Fortunately, a full moon provided ample light to care for the bull and by 1:00 a.m., we had the carcass quartered and hanging in a tree.

Packing out Mack's trophy the next day brought to an end a great first elk hunting trip for both of us.

One shot from Mack's custom 30-378 took the big bull down.

Bucks & Bulls is considered one of the West's premier big game outfitters.

BUCKS & BULLS
GUIDES & OUTFITTERS, INC.
OUTFITTER FOCUS: UTAH-NEW MEXICO

Bucks & Bulls is considered by those in the know to be one of the premier mule deer, elk and antelope outfitters in the West. Their hunts are conducted on large private leases that are strictly managed for trophy animals.

The quality of trophies they produce, as well as the professionalism with which they operate, is at a level achieved by few.

TROPHY MULE DEER HUNTS:

Maple Butte Camp

This hunt takes place on a large ranch that has a long and recent history of producing outstanding mule deer. There will be two, 5-day hunts with a maximum of six hunters in camp. One hunt will be the first week in September with the other in mid-October.

Aspen Flats Camp

This high quality ranch is always capable of producing a record class deer. Two, late October, 5-day hunts with a maximum of six hunters in camp will be offered.

Three Forks Camp

There are two times during the year when trophy bucks are vulnerable; in August when they are concentrated in their bachelor bands above timberline and during the November rut. This lease offers the opportunity to hunt trophy bucks during both these times. The two August hunts are limited to a maximum of three hunters in camp and the November hunt will be restricted to a maximum of four hunters.

(**Outfitters' notes:** *These trophy mule deer camps represent three of the finest mule deer hunts available. Please remember, however, that current and past weather conditions are a big factor in the success of our trophy deer hunts from year to year!*)

TROPHY BULL ELK HUNTS:

Maple Butte Camp

This hunt takes place on a large ranch in northern Utah that supports excellent numbers of trophy bulls. A maximum of six hunters will be accepted for each of the three, 5-day hunts.

Three Forks Camp

The Three Forks hunt takes place in mid-September during the rut. It is on private property in western Utah.

Aspen Flats Camp

This will be a first time offering on this lease at this time of year. The first week of September will be reserved for three hunters who will hunt one on one.

Dawson Camp

Dawson is a large ranch in New Mexico that produced a 412 B&C bull in 1992. One 5-day hunt will be offered on this property.

Aspen Flats Camp

This quality hunt offers many mature bulls and lots of bugling activity. Two, 5-day, September hunts are offered with a maximum of six hunters in camp.

MANAGEMENT BULL ELK HUNT:

Maple Butte Camp

There is a good number of old, 5x5 or 5x6 bulls on this ranch that, because of their genetics, will never be 6x6s. For this reason, it is the desire of the ranch management to cull these bulls from the herd. There will be one 5-day, early October hunt offered.

TROPHY ANTELOPE HUNT:

Dawson Camp

This 3-day antelope hunt takes place on a large ranch in New Mexico. It is one of the finest trophy antelope hunts and has produced several B&C heads.

Three Forks Camp

This excellent antelope hunt has the added benefit of guaranteed permits. Two, 3-day hunts will be offered with a maximum of six hunters in camp.

BUCKS & BULLS GUIDES & OUTFITTERS, INC.

Outfitter: Kim Bonnett, 270 North Main, Lindon, UT 84042, (801) 785-5050.

Method of hunting: Walking and 4x4.

Terrain: Varies on different leases, call outfitter for specifics.

Applications: Over the counter in most areas. Outfitter will send applications to all clients. It is then up to the client to secure his or her license from the game department.

Accommodations: Ranch houses, cabins and comfortable tent camps.

SOUTHERN UTAH TROPHY

By Dennis Pahlisch

I have been hunting elk and mule deer for 15 years. Over the last 12 I have concentrated mainly on elk, taking 17 bulls. Until recently, my largest was 340 B&C.

I've been applying for special hunts where my research has shown big bulls have been taken. Finally, I drew a permit for a great trophy unit in southern Utah. Being unfamiliar with the area, I contacted a taxidermist in Richfield, Utah. We worked out a hunt swap whereby he agreed to help me with my hunt if I would go with him on a Wyoming mule deer hunt.

During his preseason scouting, my partner located a huge typical 6x6. He estimated the bull, whom he named "Gunther," would score around 385 B&C. When he gave me the news, I knew Gunther was the quality

Utah holds some of the best elk habitat in the West.

of bull I had been looking for all of these years. Arriving two days before season, we began our search for the giant bull. However hunting is hunting and we never again spotted Gunther.

We located four bulls that would score over 350 B&C during our first days of hunting. With only a 340 on my wall it was very hard to let some of them go, however my partner assured me there were much bigger bulls in the area.

On the third evening of the hunt we were walking along a road when suddenly, his son came roaring up in the pickup. Jumping from the truck he exclaimed, "You didn't shoot one yet! You didn't shoot one yet!" After the young man calmed down, he told us of a giant 8x8 bull he had seen crossing a ridge only 60 yards in front of him.

That night at camp, we grabbed our note pads and began calculating the bull's possible score. When the numbers were all added up, we arrived at a possible gross score of 396 B&C!

With thoughts of the 8x8 and the sounds of bugling elk all around us, there was very little sleep in camp that night. Rising two hours before daylight, we headed to the area where the huge bull had been seen. An hour before light, I stepped from the truck, bugled, and got an immediate response from what sounded like a big bull.

Moving slowly, we worked our way up to the edge of a small lake

Dennis' giant Utah bull grossed 393 5/8 B&C.

where six bulls were working the area. To get to where the big bull was bugling, I had to sneak past four other bulls, all over 300. Cows were scattered everywhere, but somehow we managed to make our way up the ridge without spooking them.

As I approached the edge of an aspen clearing, I spotted a cow slipping through the opening 300 yards ahead. Suddenly, a big bull appeared just behind her. A quick look through my 10x70 Fujisan binoculars told me it was the 8x8 from the night before. Moving to a nearby tree, I took a rest and dropped him with one shot from my .340 Weatherby magnum, shooting 250-grain Nosler Partition bullets. The giant bull gross scored 393 5/8 and netted out 375 2/8 B&C.

Dennis' keys to success: All of my bulls have been taken on public land. Research is the number one thing that has allowed me to do this. Magazines, especially *The Eastmans' Journal*, are my major source of information. During the off season, I read as many articles as I can about elk hunting. This teaches me not only where big bulls are being taken, but also provides me with techniques other successful hunters use. If I had to choose my favorite state for hunting bull elk, hands down it would be Wyoming. Most Wyoming areas regularly produce 6-point bulls in the 280 to 300 B&C class.

Next to research, preseason scouting is the most important ingredient in a successful hunt. When I get into the field before season, I scout early in the morning and late at night. You must be careful not to disturb the elk by entering the areas where they live. I stay at least 1/2 mile away, sticking to the ridge tops where I spend a lot of time glassing to pattern the elk.

My favorite time of year to hunt elk is during the rut. If that isn't possible, I stay home until late October or early November. By then, the elk have extended their feeding times and spend more time out of the timber.

Once the hunt begins, you have to maintain a positive attitude. You won't always be lucky enough to take an animal on the first or second day. Even when things get tough, you have to drag yourself out of the sack each morning and get out there and glass. If you've done your homework, in a normal week-long hunt you'll get your opportunity.

If you want to kill a big bull, you have to be able to let the smaller ones go. You can't always shoot the first 6-point you see. On my Utah and British Colombia hunts, I had to pass on several mature bulls before I pulled the trigger. To me, just being able to see bulls like that is great. I don't always have to fill my tag for it to be a successful hunt.

WASHINGTON

Al Martz with his six-point cow elk.

WORLD RECORD COW?

BY AL MARTZ

The year I took this trophy, the elk season in northeastern Washington state ran concurrent with the deer season. I spent the week before elk season hunting deer and scouting for elk, but found no encouraging sign.

Two elk hunting friends and I hunted all of our usual areas for the first six days of the 12-day season without success. These areas are all public lands, so they receive a lot of pressure from both deer and elk hunters.

On the afternoon of the eighth day, a steady wind was blowing as I headed for a good area that is located 1 1/2 miles off the road. I thought an elk might be feeding at the bottom of the open ridge with the wind

The cow green scored 317 2/8 B&C.

141

at its back. My hunch was right. Reaching the area just before dark, I spotted a bull elk feeding at the bottom of the ridge in a patch of old ceanothus.

The elk appeared to have a good-sized rack, but since any elk with antlers in our area is a shooter, I looked only long enough to determine it was a bull. The elk was facing me with its head up, about 200 yards away. The first 180-grain Barnes X bullet from my 30-388 struck the neck, dropping the elk instantly.

It quickly regained its feet and, on wobbly legs turned and quartered away. I shot a second time and then a third before the elk dropped.

I hurried down to the animal as the light was fading and started field-dressing it from the center of the belly up to the brisket. As I turned to slit the hide in the other direction, I was surprised to find this animal had the wrong parts. I was looking at an udder. After staring at this strange animal for a couple of minutes, looking back and forth from the rack to the udder, I headed back home to get some help.

My elk had all the organs of a cow and none of a bull. It is possible she may have even had a calf, as her udder wasn't like that of a dry cow. If that's true, I would sure like to find the bull that bred her! The velvet on her rack had been shed in a normal manner and the entire rack was completely clean and dark.

I aged my elk at 7 1/2 years and estimated her live weight to be 775 pounds. Her feet were small for an elk of this size, and though her head and neck measured to the size of a large bull, she did not have the mane of a bull.

I have talked to people at the R.M.E.F., Boone and Crockett Club and six other biologists. As far as anyone knows, it is unheard of for a cow elk to have anymore than a spike or a raghorn rack at best, let alone a 6x6 that nets 317 2/8 B&C green. I wish there were records for animals like this, I probably have a World Record Cow!

THREE SIXES

By Bill Phifer

As you can see from these photos, it's been another good year. None of my bulls were of record-book quality, but three 6-point bulls in one year can't possibly qualify as bad.

My first elk of the year was taken in western Wyoming during archery season. He is a young bull without much mass or length, but fine eating. I spent 15 minutes within 30 yards of this bull, trying to decide if I should pass, especially since the herd bull in the area would have easily scored 325 P&Y. However, when the smaller bull finally fed broadside to me at 15 yards, I felt it was pushing my luck to let him go. This was the second day of the hunt, and of course I saw two other bulls in excess of 300 points later in the week (one at less than 25 yards). My partner took a young bull from that herd.

The following week, we hunted in Montana, using my llamas to pack in and set up a base camp about five miles from the trailhead. We experienced light snow and bitter cold the first couple of days, not that unusual for the high country in mid-September, but not exactly welcome either. I passed on a spike and 5-point early, but we were seeing very few elk.

Late on the fourth day of the hunt, I spotted a herd and carefully worked in among the cows. The bull was really fired up, but I had trouble seeing him due to the ridgeline blocking my view. I spent 20 minutes with calves running around me and one cow grazing at four yards until finally the bull broke over the top and followed a yearling cow right into the open in front of me. As I came to full draw, he stopped at 12 yards, momentarily forgetting the hot cow he was pursuing. After the shot, the bull traveled only about 200 yards over the ridge before expiring. During all the excitement, another nice 6-point showed up and made off with my bull's cows.

My Montana bull had broken his brow tine off at the main beam on the right side, and all the other tines had lost an inch or two in battle, adding real character to the rack. He scores right at 310 P&Y and was aged by the local biologist at 12 to 15 years old. His teeth were down to

This bull was taken by Bill in Wyoming.

the gum line with the molars worn completely smooth. I packed the boned meat out to the road on three of my llamas while my partner continued hunting.

The third bull was taken the first week of October in a limited-draw unit on the Washington coast. This was a fabulous unit in which I counted over 130 bulls in three days of hunting, though most were juveniles and raghorn 4- and 5-points. One large herd across from my camp held over 80 head of which 34 were bulls! This country was heavily logged and uncharacteristically open for Roosevelt elk, but the extremely limited permit system has certainly produced plenty of elk, even if very few were large. There was no noticeable rutting activity during my hunt as numerous bulls mingled with the cows.

I had my sights set on taking a bull with crown points, whereas most of the elk had more typical racks reminiscent of small Rocky Mountain elk. I worked within 175 yards of this bull after spotting him through the rain and fog on the third day of the hunt. The bull quickly bedded in a small patch of timber while the rest of the herd stayed in the open, resulting in a three-hour wait until he presented a shot. He soaked up three perfectly-placed 180-grain Noslers before going down, almost making me wish for a bow again. I was able to drive within 75 yards of this bull making him by far the easiest pack trip I've had in quite a while!

Above: The antlers on Bill's Montana bull have lots of character.

Left: Bill's Washington bull was an easy pack, falling only 75 yards from the road.

W Y O M I N G

WYOMING RECORD BULL ELK

Merwyn Martin is a true trophy hunter from Powell, Wyoming. His bull officially scored 412 B&C, which ties it with the second-largest elk ever recorded in Wyoming. The largest taken in Wyoming scores 441 6/8 and was taken in the Big Horn Mountains in 1890. The second place elk with the same score as Martin's was killed in 1886.

How many years have you applied for a license in Area 51?
The desire really began 18 years ago, but I've really hunted in earnest for the last 10. I've spent a lot of time and money hunting this kind of bull. I didn't really intend to kill a B&C bull—I just wanted a nice 6-point to put on the wall. I've drawn permits that have gone unfilled because I couldn't find the bull I was looking for. To fill the freezer, my wife applies for a cow permit, and if we fill it, my permit is released for a trophy hunt. So although I've drawn permits for years and had many opportunities, I've often come out of the hills with an unfilled tag. I never felt I had to kill something.

How did this particular hunt go?
The week before the late bull season began in mid-November, the weather turned exceptionally cold, pushing game out of the high country earlier than usual. There were no hunters to stop them.

During the week between seasons, I was deer hunting when I spotted this bull running with seven others. Five nice bulls were in the bunch, but this bull dwarfed them all. Unfortunately, the season wouldn't open for another seven days.

Two friends with cow permits agreed to keep an eye on him for me. They'd seen him come out on the same ridge two nights in a row but the odds he'd be there opening morning were slim. My best chance of ambushing him was to get up the mountain and on the ridge before daylight. On opening morning, I returned with a flashlight at 4:00 o'clock to begin my climb.

When I arrived at my destination, my clothes were soaked with perspiration. By then, it was snowing so hard I couldn't see more than 50 yards. Six inches of new, wet snow added to my already wet clothing, made me a prime candidate for hypothermia. I decided to return to camp for dry clothing and some lunch.

The weather cleared about 10:00 a.m. and I began to ponder the situation. I knew the bull wouldn't come out on that ridge due to the fresh snow. I figured he'd be in one of the lower basins that night so I prepared a plan of action that paid off.

I spotted him feeding on a plateau about 3:30 that afternoon. To get to the bull, I had to climb back out of the canyon and circle behind him. It took nearly an hour and by then the bull had moved. Following his tracks, I headed into the timber and walked right up on him, startling both of us. He was only 50 yards away when he threw his head up and looked at me. There was no question in my mind that he was the one I was looking for.

For once in my life, I did everything right. When he gave me the opportunity, I was ready to go. The first shot wasn't good because he was quartered and looking at me. He was hit hard and staggered, but didn't go down. I chambered the second round. Now he was looking straight at me and I don't like that kind of shot because I'm not a good off-hand shot.

Suddenly, the shadow of another bull appeared. At the movement, the huge bull turned his head, giving me a better shot at his shoulder. The shot hit him hard, but he still didn't go down. I was shooting a .270 Weatherby magnum loaded with Nosler 150-grain Partition bullets. It blew my mind that the bull was not on the ground. As I quickly chambered the third round, he turned broadside and I put him down.

When I walked over to him, I knew I had killed a big bull! I'm sure you could have heard me hollering 50 miles away if you had been listening. It was quite a thrill, no doubt about it. One of hardest things I've ever had to do was leave him on the mountain that night. I couldn't get him out by myself so I dressed and caped him, then returned to my truck by flashlight.

I hardly slept all night, worrying about coyotes tearing up the cape. After getting some help, I was back to the kill site at daylight. It took three of us over 5 1/2 hours to get my bull out of that hole. We couldn't get a horse to him, so we took him out by block and tackle.

Why had so many elk migrated into this area?

I think it was a combination of two things. First, we had a lot of moisture, producing good vegetation. Second, we had an early blast of extremely cold weather to push them out. Like most hunters trying to get a good trophy, I've spent a lot of time studying game to see what moves them around. I've always said it isn't the snow that moves the game as much as below-zero temperatures. To me, 10 degrees below zero is the magic number.

When I was staying in my cabin during deer season and the weather dipped below zero two or three nights, I saw more bull elk than I had ever seen in my life.

Do they winter right there?

Yes, it's their normal wintering grounds.

Have you taken other nice bulls?

No, I've only killed one other respectable 5-point. Between then and now, I've taken several smaller bulls, but this is the first really nice bull I've ever harvested. In fact, I haven't filled my tag for the last four years. I never dreamed of or cared about getting a B&C head. I was trying to get a bull that would score around 340 to hang on the wall of my cabin, then I'd go back to being a meat hunter for the rest of my life. I spent a lot of time trying to get this bull and he was beyond my wildest dreams.

My taxidermist, Jim Marsico, green scored the 8x7 bull at 418 7/8 inches. He officially scored 412 B&C. His main beams measures 61 3/8 inches, royal 27 2/8 inches, spread 50 6/8 inches, and the height 60 inches. His rack weighs more than 44 pounds.

It took three days for me to comprehend the size of this bull. When Jim proved with the B&C Record Book that my bull could very well be the largest killed in Wyoming since 1890, it started to come home. Yes, I had killed a really big bull.

What are you going to do with him after he's mounted?

I'll probably display him with the Boone and Crockett Collection at the Buffalo Bill Museum in Cody.

What do you do for a living?

I'm a concrete contractor, which is one reason I've always tried to draw this late permit. After it turns cold, my work slows down enough to allow me time to go hunting. I don't have much opportunity to hunt early in the season.

I've lived in Powell all my life. Sometimes we've put up with some starving-to-death situations, but I've always loved to hunt and fish and that's kept me here. Some of the magic behind this bull is the fact that I am a Wyoming native. In fact, I took my first elk in the same area when I was 15 years old. I know the animals' habits and the area. I have learned a little bit more every year and this year, I just put it all together.

(***Author's notes:*** *Draw Area 51 is not known for being an excellent big bull area, but it is a decent one. Early snows pull some good bulls out of Yellowstone Park only about once every 15 years.*)

Gary alongside his B&C nontypical trophy bull.

A BULL WORTH WAITING FOR

BY JIM TALLEY

While hunting in central Wyoming, Gary Pagel of Pound, Wisconsin, took a nontypical bull elk that will place his name in the prestigious Boone and Crockett Record Book.

Gary and his father, Richard, began applying for elk tags in the area after a relative reported seeing large bulls there while antelope hunting. After three years of trying, luck was with them as the Pagels drew the long-awaited tags and booked a guided hunt for the second week of the season.

The father and son spent a lot of time and effort preparing for their Wyoming hunt. Gary worked up hand-loads for his custom .300 Weatherby, using Trophy Bonded Bear Claw bullets. In anticipation of cold weather and snow, Gary and Richard purchased Schnees pacs. Also, Gary outfitted himself with clothing from King Of The Mountain Wool. Gary believes in using the best equipment available and his choice of top-notch gear enables him to hunt comfortably in any weather.

When the two hunters arrived in Wyoming, the November weather was unseasonably warm. The first days were uneventful until the last hour of the third evening, when Richard and his guide, Mike Wakkuri, spotted some elk at a long distance. They were able to move within range just as shooting light faded and Richard made a great shot, dropping a nice 6-point. By the time they reached the bull, a flash was required for taking photographs.

Gary hoped to find a bull at least as nice as Richard's, and with two days left to hunt, they received the foot of snow they had been hoping for.

The next morning, the hunters cut fresh tracks that appeared to be those of two bulls and eight cows and calves. Gary and Mike followed them across several big, open parks until finally spotting the elk in a strip of timber 400 yards away. Seeing only cows, they decided to make a big circle to keep the wind in their favor. As they stalked closer, Gary suddenly spotted a big bull at 60 yards. There was no need to look further!

Four solid hits from the Weatherby were required to put the elk on

153

Main beam circumferences on Gary's bull average eight inches.

the ground. Any one of the four would have been fatal—the big bull just refused to go down.

The massive 6x7 nontypical rack and skull plate were unbelievably heavy and the circumferences on the main beams average close to eight inches. The inside spread on Gary's bull measured an incredible 57 inches. With a B&C green score of well over 400 inches, and a net of 395 2/8 nontypical, this was certainly a bull worth waiting for.

(***Notes:*** *Gary and Richard hunted with Myron and Mike Wakkuri, owners of Elk Mountain Outfitters in Wheatland, WY, (307) 322-3220. The Wakkuris offer antelope, whitetail, mule deer and elk hunts on private land. They also guide for bighorn sheep.*

Besides qualifying for B&C, Gary's bull should also rank in the top five under the SCI system.)

350 WYOMING BULL

BY LARRY BAUGHMAN

This is a photo of the elk my brother, Alva, harvested on a November hunt in Wyoming. The bull gross scored 350 6/8 B&C. It has 51-inch main beams with a 43-inch inside spread. Total deductions on the bull, Alva's first, were only 5 2/8 inches.

Linda and her trophy in front of the magnificent Teton Mountains.

Teton Park Trophy

By Linda Grivet

I had never hunted before moving to Wyoming from Iowa 15 years ago. My husband is a great teacher, however, and now I love to hunt big game. This bull was taken after I drew a special elk permit for Wyoming's Grand Teton Park. These tags are highly sought-after, due to the quality of bulls that migrate through the area.

When we arrived in Jackson for our October hunt, the area had yet to receive snow and the ground was bare. Prior to this year's hunt, I had only taken one bull elk, a 5-point. Now, I hoped to get a chance at a big bull.

Early on the morning of October 18, my husband dropped me in the area I planned to hunt. As I walked toward the Snake River, I spotted my bull along with two others feeding in the sagebrush. They were moving and I really didn't have time to judge them accurately, but I could tell all three were very respectable bulls.

My bull stopped, turned broadside, and I dropped him with my 30-06. Another hunter later harvested one of the remaining bulls, a non-typical 7-point. We packed my bull out in two trips using a wheeled cart. He officially scores 344 B&C. Since our ceilings are too low to accommodate a shoulder mount, I mounted only the antlers.

I wasn't the only one in our home to have a great year. My husband drew a Wyoming moose permit and took a Boone and Crockett bull. It will definitely be tough to top this year of hunting.

We both work in a coal mine and use most of our vacation time to hunt. We first learned about *The Eastmans' Journal* when a friend who is a subscriber showed my husband his most recent copy. Being such avid trophy hunters, we wasted no time in subscribing.

*(**Notes:** The holder of a Teton Park permit has the opportunity to hunt for huge Yellowstone bulls. However, hunting success is largely dependent upon the weather. If enough snow accumulates, the Yellowstone elk migrate through this area during the hunting season. Hunting can be very tough on a dry year, though Linda proved it is still possible to take a good bull.)*

Above: Linda Lacitinola with her first bull elk.

Right: Robert's arrow found its mark at a distance of only 13 yards.

BUGLING WYOMING BULLS

BY ROBERT D. LACITINOLA, JR.

Hunting elk with a bow has to be one of the most exciting experiences a hunter can have. I shot this bull at 13 yards. To be so close to an animal that big is really something.

The archery elk season opened in early September near my home in northeastern Wyoming. The first day began with much promise. Within the first 30 minutes of hunting, an average 5-point bull was on his way up the trail in response to my cow calls. This was to be my first elk, so I wasn't going to be too picky.

Just as I was thinking how easy it was going to be this year, I noticed a little problem. The bull was coming slightly uphill and to my left, which was fine except that I was still standing on the trail. He was just 40 yards away when I first spotted him, and I hadn't had time to move into position for a shot. One of the real challenges in archery elk hunting is guessing which way a bull is going to come in.

This time, I guessed wrong. Instead of angling to my left, he decided to come straight into my position behind a small pine tree. Within seconds we were eye to eye at 11 yards, with the bull quartering sharply toward me offering no chance for a shot. After a brief stand-off, he melted into the timber and was gone. So much for an easy hunt, but what a great way to begin the season.

The next several days were filled with snowstorms, hail storms, high winds and close calls with bulls. Still, an unfilled elk tag remained in my pack. The high country in September is completely unpredictable when it comes to the weather. I have left camp in a T-shirt at daybreak only to return in the evening during a snowstorm. Needless to say, I never leave camp without being prepared for foul weather.

The next to the last evening of the hunt found my wife and me working a bull in the timber. We figured if I could bugle the bull in close, Linda could cow call him past me so that I could get a shot. The bull bugled over and over, but wouldn't come in. After setting up on him several times, I decided I had to get closer than usual before calling him in for a shot.

I headed down the hill toward the elk, sneaking in as close as I dared before starting to bugle and cow call. The strategy worked and in he came. I'll never forget when he bugled at 30 yards, then closed the distance to 13 yards where my arrow found its mark. I had hunted hard for 10 straight days and was fortunate to take my first elk the day before I had to return to work.

Mule deer season opened in early October. After a short hunt with a friend, my tag was filled, and it was Linda's turn.

My wife's first day of mule deer hunting was long, with much trial and error but she was able to take a buck. I encouraged her by explaining she wasn't the first one to miss a mulie in open country. We hoped her elk area would offer shooting from a much closer range.

Linda had a tag for a hard-to-draw limited-entry area. Our scouting revealed plenty of elk sign, and we both felt she would have a good chance of harvesting a decent bull.

When opening day finally arrived, we were both very excited. I was armed with our video camera, while Linda carried her 7mm-08 Remington. Shortly after leaving the main road, we heard a bull bugling in the timber. Unfortunately, I had left my bugle hanging on the handle bars of my ATV, so we weren't able to pinpoint the bull's location.

After 90 minutes of hiking, we reached a small meadow we had scouted earlier. Fresh sign was abundant in the timber and the meadow as Linda slipped into the small blind we had built.

While my wife settled into the blind, I chose to continue walking for about 40 yards so that I could watch a trail-covered area she was unable see. I figured if I spotted an elk, I could signal to Linda and hopefully, she could get a shot. As the snow began to fall, I moved to the shelter of an overhanging pine tree to wait.

Just as I was getting comfortable, the first shot rang out. I jumped to my feet and ran through the woods toward Linda. When I spotted her, she was looking through her rifle scope toward the far end of the meadow. Following her line of sight, I saw a bull elk standing with his front legs spread wide to hold himself upright. Even though he appeared to be hit hard, I yelled for Linda to shoot again. The words had barely left my mouth when the second shot hit him. The bull took two steps and went down for good.

That year was truly a season to remember for Linda and me. Not only did we both fill out on mule deer, but we were able to share the excitement as each of us took our first elk.

FIRST ELK GOES
POPE AND YOUNG

BY PAUL JAKOVAC

My first successful elk hunt took place in the Medicine Bow National Forest just west of Laramie, Wyoming. If I had made it up, the story couldn't be better!

After five unsuccessful years of rifle elk hunting, I decided to hunt with my bow. I was a fourth year Wildlife Management student at the University of Wyoming and knew I would be able to devote more time to hunting in September than later in the fall.

During the past two years I have been learning more and more about elk from my friend, Alan Sinner. From him came my knowledge that the best places to find elk include the edges of meadows and clear cuts that are surrounded by timber. These provide excellent feeding areas during the low-light hours. The elk will use springs and creek drainages for wallows and they like to bed on timbered benches.

Alan taught me to identify the sex of an elk by the feces dropped in the fall. A bull will have a pit on one side of the pellet. I also learned how to use topographical maps to my advantage.

Wind direction is an important consideration, not only while hunting, but also when scouting an area. Generally, the thermals will blow down the valleys in the morning and then reverse directions in the afternoon. The most important lesson I learned from Alan was that no matter what I had read or heard, elk will be where you find them.

Armed with my knowledge and seven-and-a-half- minute topographical maps, I began to study the area. Archery season would open on September 1, so I began scouting in late August.

During my scouting, two small creek drainages with scattered meadows caught my eye. Further investigation revealed numerous droppings and fresh tracks.

When I returned to the area on opening morning, I heard a bugle. I called back, but the bull didn't want anything to do with me. The area was under heavy pressure from other hunters, so I decided to look elsewhere.

161

Paul's first bull elk net scored 312 P&Y.

While exploring another drainage a week later, I carelessly jumped a dozen cows and one bull. They were really spooked, so I decided to return the next morning.

The following day, I started up the trail 30 minutes before daylight. When I reached the spot where I had jumped the elk the night before, there was a camp set up. Even though I was discouraged, I headed up the ridge in hopes of not disturbing the other hunter.

When I reached the top, I found a large meadow with lots of elk sign and many fresh wallows. After a short wait, I heard the faint call of a bull elk in the distance. Following the sound of the call, I moved about a half mile farther into the timber until I reached a second meadow.

As I rested, a loud squeal came from the timber. The bull was only about 125 to 150 yards away! My heart pounded faster and harder as we bugled back and forth for the next 30 minutes. I knew it would be difficult to draw the bull out of the timber so I decided to move in on him.

After checking the wind direction, I began my stalk. By moving cautiously around the meadow only when the bull bugled, I was able to keep track of his exact location. The sound of his bugle also helped cover any noise I made as I slipped through the timber.

I crept along until I reached a large tree to use as cover. As I was setting up, he bugled again from 40 yards away. I answered immediately. When I peeked around the tree, I saw his left antler less than 20 yards from me. I pulled back, but couldn't resist a second look. The bull was at 10 yards and still moving slowly in my direction. I drew my bow and waited.

My heart was beating so hard, I'm sure the elk couldn't help hearing it. When he came into my line of vision, he was only four yards away! I nearly died when he spooked and then stopped out of sight about 20 yards away. The bull bugled again, then started moving uphill to my left.

Unfortunately for him, he stopped broadside, giving me a clear shot. I stuck my arrow behind his left shoulder...a good, clean hit that caught both lungs!

I found him after following the blood trail for 30 minutes. He had run only about 100 yards before going down. As I dressed the bull, I began to worry about how I was going to pack him over three miles to my truck.

While packing out the first load of elk meat, I ran into another hunter at the camp I had passed on the way in. He offered to help, and nine hours after the kill we had the bull loaded in the truck.

My first elk has six points on each side with 46-inch main beams. He officially grossed 316 7/8 P&Y with a final net of 312 P&Y. I took him using a Darton Excel bow and 125-grain Rocky Mountain broadheads.

I would like to extend a special thanks to the following:

Carlos Ochoa—I would still be packing if it weren't for you.

Alan Sinner—if it wasn't for your help, I would still have a tag to fill.

God—thank you for answering my prayers.

Ron Dube provides a first-class wilderness experience for his clients.

OUTFITTER FOCUS

RON DUBE'S WILDERNESS ADVENTURES WYOMING ELK HUNT

BY LEE JOHNSON

After applying and failing to draw for deer, elk and sheep in five states, it didn't take much convincing when my good friend, Jim O'Neal, asked me to tag along with him and his son, Jimmy, on their elk hunt. The hunt was to take place near Wyoming's Yellowstone Park with outfitter Ron Dube's Wilderness Adventures. Ron, who is extremely well organized and knowledgeable, hunts one of the best areas in the West.

We arrived in Cody, Wyoming on September 9 after a beautiful morning drive through Grand Teton and Yellowstone National Parks. Guide Mike Fitzgerald, along with Ron's wife, Carol, met us at the historic Irma Hotel. After introductions and paperwork, it was off to the local range to make sure the rifles were still properly zeroed.

After a tour of the Buffalo Bill Museum, which is definitely a must-see in Cody, we settled in at the Irma with high expectations. Thundershowers most of the night left us with a picture-perfect day for the eight-hour horseback ride into Ron's Mountain Creek Camp.

We arrived in camp at 6:00 p.m. for hors d'oeuvres followed by dinner and an excellent briefing by our outfitter. Ron lets everyone know up front what's expected of them and what they can expect. His advice was that if you wanted to be sure of tagging an elk, shoot the first 5-point or better.

Despite the large camp, we found elk nearby as we hiked out of camp early the next morning. Before shooting light, we heard bulls bugling from three different locations. Ron picked the one that sounded the largest and we went after him. As we hurried along, the bull suddenly bugled 100 yards ahead. It sounded as if he was heading right for us. Sneaking through the thick timber on the edge of a large meadow we continued in the direction of the elk.

Just as Jimmy was climbing over a large deadfall, the bull appeared.

Jim O'Neal's Wyoming bull green scored 350 B&C.

When Jim saw the length of the tines, he didn't wait to count points. At 50 yards, he saw a small opening to the vitals and the .300 Weatherby magnum, custom Mountain Rifle dropped the 350 B&C bull in its tracks. We couldn't believe the size of the massively heavy rack and how fast everything happened.

After taking care of Jim's bull, the wranglers packed it back to camp and we continued with our hunt. There was fresh sign everywhere as many elk had been living in this timber. We covered numerous miles that day and bugled to several bulls. One good bull came to us but this was Jimmy's first elk hunt and he wasn't as quick as his dad. It was well after dark when we arrived back at camp with that tired, contented feeling that comes only from a tough but successful day of hunting.

The second day, Ron, Jimmy and I set out on foot again for some more great country. At 10:00 a.m., we spotted a herd of 15 elk that included a huge 6x7. They were about a mile away and we watched them out in the open for an hour before they went over a ridge into some timber.

After waiting for the wind to change, we tried to put the sneak on them but found they had traveled two drainages over. Later, another of Ron's hunters found the 6x7 bedded and killed him at 350 yards with his .300 Weatherby.

We hunted hard every day and had elk bugling each morning and evening. The weather was warm and clear, shutting down the rut during the day. We came close to getting a bull for Jimmy but something always seemed to go wrong. One morning a bull came right in to the sounds of our horses but it was still dark and he spooked. Another morning, the only other hunters within 20 miles killed two nice bulls right under our noses.

This hunt was a tremendous experience. In addition to all the elk, we were able to glass bighorn sheep every day. Jim spotted a black bear, but we saw no grizzlies, though their fresh sign was everywhere and one claimed the gut pile of Jim's elk. The scene of Jim's kill two days later was an awesome testament to the power of the grizzly. It looked like a tractor had buried what was left of the elk.

Ron runs one of the finest hunting camps you'll find anywhere.

Ron Dube is one heck of an outfitter. He knows the country and the animals, and has the drive to be successful.

Ron and Carol Dube have an excellent reputation for running a first-class operation. Besides their hunting camps, they also provide summer pack trips into the Washakie Wilderness near Cody, Wyoming.

Be sure to inquire about Wilderness Adventures' late-season trophy mule deer hunts. These offer the opportunity to hunt bucks as they migrate toward their winter range. Ron emphasizes there are not book deer behind every tree but some good trophies are always taken on these hunts.

Contact: Ron & Carol Dube, P.O. Box 167, Wapiti, WY 82450, Ph. (307) 527-7815.

Heading up the snow-covered trail with the Akersons.

WYOMING WILDERNESS BULL

BY ED AKERSON

After years of talking about the "grand tour" elk hunt, we finally decided to stop the talk and walk the walk. There is a 130-mile section of wilderness trails we had always wanted to see and a September hunt seemed like a good way to do it. The bulls would be bugling and the hunting would be good.

My wife, Jackie, and I purchased general resident elk tags while our brother-in-law, Roger Peterson, of Fairburn, South Dakota, had drawn a nonresident general tag. Jackie's dad, Jack Smith, would be going along just to see the spectacular Thorofare country and the Yellowstone River. Rounding out the party were good friends Bob and Lil Ennist who had resident general elk tags and their brother-in-law, Steve Erick, of Bellefountaine, Ohio, who had also drawn a nonresident general elk tag.

It was quite a sight as we headed up the trail with 18 head of horses, including 11 just for packing! After seven hours of riding and a few sore body parts, we made camp for the first night.

The next morning Roger and I headed into a basin to glass, but all we saw were horse tracks. Moving into another basin that afternoon we spotted bighorn sheep so high up on the cliffs it makes you wonder how they ever got there. It is sights like those that keep you applying for one of those big old rams. Someday, maybe—

Meanwhile, Bob and Steve had located three small bulls but we had all decided to hold out for something bigger. Steve had the honor of seeing a sow grizzly with two cubs. Jackie had scared the bears from the timber high above camp while still-hunting with her .50-caliber Hawkins.

After a good supper, we all hit the sack so we could bug out early the next morning. We planned for two people to hunt in the morning while the others broke camp and saddled the horses. That evening, two others would hunt while the rest of the crew set up camp again.

On the third morning there were elk bugling all around us. Roger and I put the sneak on three bulls, but the big 6-point we wanted would not come off a high bench. As the temperature rose, the bulls quieted down and disappeared into the thick, dark timber.

On the way back to camp we walked up on a big 48-inch moose with long points and huge palms. Again, I wished I had been lucky enough to draw a moose tag.

The next day we repeated our leap-frog hunting and moving performance. As we moved through the timber burned by the Yellowstone fires of 1988, the drizzle and fog set in. That night when we made camp everyone was very excited as the weather began to worsen. We all knew the hunting was about to get a whole lot better.

After riding 54 miles, Jack was amazed at the size of the Thorofare country. He figured you could put all the Black Hills inside this wilderness and never find them again!

Roger and I were into elk again the following morning but still no big bulls. We were also into grizzlies as one had run off seven head of horses. Fortunately, the picket ropes became tangled and we were able to catch the strays before they completely left the country.

Heavy snow was falling as we headed toward our next campsite. The layer of fresh snow made everything perfectly quiet as we moved up the trail. Topping a rise, I saw three cows in the trail ahead. We stopped and glassed the area, then moved on. However, just around the next corner, I spotted a bull pawing in the snow 100 yards ahead.

I raised my hand and motioned to Roger, who was directly behind my three pack horses. He bailed off his horse and eased up to a perfect gun rock 15 yards in front of me. After what seemed like an eternity, Roger turned and whispered that he wanted a bigger bull. Steve had hurried up to the front of the string by then and saw the heavy antlered 5-point. He had hunted elk once before and knew the slim odds of shooting a good bull. Leaning across the rock, Steve let a bullet fly. The bull spun and ran 40 yards before dropping beside the trail.

After all the handshakes and congratulations, Bob and Steve headed down to field dress the elk while the rest of our party set out to find a place to camp. We told Bob and Steve to follow our tracks in the snow until they smelled the coffee!

We hadn't gone far when we spotted a herd of 30 elk that included three satellite bulls and one big 6-point. It was almost sundown and the snow really started to fall as Roger began his stalk. He managed to get off one shot but unfortunately, it didn't connect. The elk were not spooked so we decided to back off and return the following day.

The next morning found Bob, Roger and me sneaking into a canyon looking for the 6-point we had seen the night before. Soon, I spotted a bull looking at us through a stand of timber 500 yards away. Roger and

*Above: Jackie Akerson
with her wilderness bull.*

*Left: The Ackersons
hunted in the area
where the Yellowstone
fires of 1988 burned.*

Bob stayed by the horses while I moved closer. Slipping into a small group of trees, I bugled once. The bull answered immediately, parting the trees with his antlers as he stormed out to guard the cows.

The whole hillside seemed to come alive with elk! I bugled one more time and the 6-point charged another 50 yards in my direction. Placing the crosshairs of my .300 Weatherby magnum on his chest, I popped a cap. The report was solid, but unbelievably the bull turned to walk away. My second shot was a clean jerk of the trigger.

As I watched the bull disappear over the ridge, I felt sick. I knew I had hit him with the first shot but now he was heading for a deep, dark hole Bob and I had been in several years before.

Thirty minutes later, as I topped the ridge where the bull had disappeared, he suddenly appeared 40 yards in front of me. I raised the Weatherby and fired again, aiming for the heart and lungs. The bull turned, ran down a finger and dropped on the last bench before that dark hole of a canyon.

Roger and Bob brought the horses around and we quartered the elk and hung him in a nearby tree for the night. Returning by way of the bull Steve had shot, we found Jackie and Steve lashing the meat tight to the panniers for the ride to camp. We were all excited about having one bull on the pack mules and another 6-point hanging a few miles away.

As we rode into camp, Jack suddenly appeared from behind the tent motioning for us to be quiet. He had been watching a bull elk on the far hillside 700 yards away. The bull would graze for a few minutes and then bugle at our horses picketed in the meadow. The adrenaline was really running now! Jackie grabbed her .270 leaving the black powder rifle behind because of wet powder problems. She sneaked to the trees 70 yards below camp and came face to face with the bugling bull. Two shots later and he was down, making a three-elk total for the camp in the last two days.

Roger couldn't stand to stay in camp so he and Bob went out for the evening hunt to try to calm their nerves. Jackie, Steve and I quartered her elk and packed it into camp. We had just settled down to rest before starting supper when we heard the report of Roger's .300 H&H magnum.

A couple of hours later, Roger and Bob arrived back in camp with a heavy 5-point bull and an incredible story. They had sat down to glass a sparsely timbered hillside when they sighted a cow in a basin directly below them. Bob let out a bugle and a bull answered back from over the canyon's edge. Five minutes later Bob bugled again. The bull answered right away—he was coming in hot and fast.

They were watching the clearing 150 yards in front of them when

Hunters l-r, Jack, Jackie, Roger, Bob, Steve and Ed.

Eighteen head of horses were required for the pack trip.

they heard the snap of a twig from behind. Bob slowly turned to see the big bull only 15 paces away, staring straight at them. Roger spun and fired, hitting the elk square in the chest. The bull ran 20 yards and collapsed. Roger swears he had to shoot in self-defense!

The next morning we boned out the meat and started the 44-mile ride back to the comfort of a Ford pickup seat. It was a great feeling coming out of God's country, our packs heavy with horn and meat. This was a trip that gave us everything we dreamed it would be and more— 10 days of pure mountain living with family and friends.

(*Ed's comments: Jackie and I enjoy* The Eastmans' Journal *more than any other magazine. It is always a fight to see who gets to read it first! When we show a copy to our friends, they all want to take it home and read it. However, we have to tell them to subscribe for themselves, we collect the magazine to put away and read on indoor days.*)

Northwest Wyoming Outfitters
Ron Dube
(307) 527-7815
P.O. Box 167
Wapiti, WY 82450

Triangle X Ranch
(307) 733-2183
Moose, WY 83012

John R. Winter
(307) 543-2309
P.O. 182
Moran, WY 83013

Dave Segall
(307) 587-4410
P.O. Box 2167
Cody, WY 82414

Warren Fleming
(307) 486-2308
P.O. Box 554
Crowheart, WY 82512

Note: *This list must be considered a service rather than an endorsement. Always check all outfitters' references.*

This bull scored 360 gross P&Y.

ELK VOCALIZATION

BY RALPH "ABE" MELINE

Notes: The following chapter is from an interview with Ralph "Abe" Meline, owner and founder of Abe & Son Natural Elk Sounds (1-800-426-2417). Abe is truly one of the pioneers in the study of elk vocalization. His call produces perhaps the most realistic variety of elk sounds of any product on the market today. Abe, a former timber cutter, has spent his life in the outdoors. He is arguably the leading expert on elk vocalization in the country having taken 37 bulls with his bow.

In The Beginning

If you don't have the right bugle, you can't really talk to the elk. You just make a sound and when bulls get close, they know it's not real and they're not going to stick around. Their heads come up and their body posture changes. They look at each other as if to say, "Do you believe that George? Let's get out of here!" Forget the herd bull, he won't have anything to do with you, he's over there tending to business.

Years ago when I started working on my elk call, many ideas were discarded along the way because to me, they just didn't produce the right sound for an elk call. I continued to work on the call every chance I got in between jobs as a timber cutter. Each year the product became more and more refined until finally, I got it down to an absolute science. (The first year I went to New Mexico with this call, we called in and killed a 409 B&C bull!)

As I learned to do more sounds and developed new techniques and more strategies, everything just fell into place and I had it where I wanted it. I put it all together and got the darn thing patented. I thought all I had to do was put out a few advertisements and the money would come rolling in. Guess what happened? The call was so good that for the first two years, everyone kept it quiet. Guys didn't even want their friends to know about this call. Fortunately, as the years passed, the word finally got out until now the call is used by hunters across the United States and Canada.

Locating and Hunting Early Season Bulls

If you pull into a new area that holds some big bulls, chances are there aren't going to be many people who will want to divulge their secrets to you. It's kind of a hushed up thing! The first thing I do is look at topo maps, look at the terrain, and then if possible, I'll just hoof it off down in the area to look around.

I'll make a few big circles down some canyons and up through some basins. If it's late August, you're looking for the rub trees up on the higher points where the cool breezes blow. That's where the bulls will be rubbing off their velvet. After you find that velvet sign, then start moving down country closer to the seeps. There is more dampness down there and the feed is better. (Vegetation is already starting to dry out on the higher more exposed points.) Pay close attention to the sign around the seeps and lush feeding areas. How the elk are behaving will depend a lot on the weather, (temperature, moisture, etc.).

When locating bulls, I used to get into a lot of strong, high note bugles that the bulls would answer. Eventually, I learned that it was better to back off on those strong bugles early in the year. I learned to be more friendly (with my bugle). Early in the fall, all an elk wants to do is take a look at you, (thinking you're another elk). If you call with a friendly, non-threatening tone, the elk will be friendly to you. I try to say to the elk what they're expecting to hear from their friends.

Some hunters may not understand what I mean by a friendly bugle. I just want to let the elk know I'm there, I'm not fluting, not shrieking or loud. I'm non-threatening.

Positioning is very important when bugling for elk. I never call from a high point. I'll bugle from a saddle or down on the side of a hill where the elk have been traveling back and forth to their feeding and bedding grounds. I just put out an easy bugle that says, "Here I am, I'm new." Then, I may throw in a couple of cow calls just to let the other bulls know I have a few girls with me.

Depending on the conditions and the area you're hunting, a bull will usually come into a friendly bugle followed by the cow calls. You have to be patient, but don't stay in one position. Move about 100 yards and call again. I throw in a lot of little calf chirps and subtle cow sounds. These are the herd sounds of cows tending their babies. It says the herd is at ease.

You have to be subtle in this situation. You're not pushing anything but you're not moving away…you're not excited. This type of vocalization doesn't have to be loud. You're supposed to be close, watching the wind, watching the terrain. I use "Baers Feet" to help me move along quietly. (These are Polarfleece booties that fit over the top of your hunt-

178

ing boots. This excellent product is available from Cabela's.)

Often, hunters will be stingy when applying a cover scent. Don't be, I pour it on! Cow scent on one foot and bull scent on the other. I call this "walking in elk smell."

When I'm traveling the elk's terrain, I'm not rubbing on their trees and I'm not urinating in their paths. When I urinate, I go off the trail where the elk haven't been walking, kick a hole in the ground and relieve myself there.

How bulls react early in the season depends on the area being hunted. The bulls down in southern Colorado and New Mexico will act differently from the bulls farther north. It's a whole different terrain down there in the cedars. I've called in those bulls in late August. They came in with velvet hanging like dishrags on their antlers.

You talk friendly and bulls will answer you, but if you aren't saying what they want to hear, they won't say anything. Usually, they won't respond to a diaphragm. Using my call, they'll talk to you because they believe you're real. There is no phoniness in that call and even experienced hunters have to listen real close to tell it from the real thing.

The Peak Of The Rut

If you have people bothering an area, bumping an area (stinking it up, I call it), then you got to get in the elk more quickly and behave in a more aggressive manner. By this time, you will know where the bulls are concentrated and you have to be careful when working in on them. I don't go right into their pocket, I circle and tease them from the perimeter. I let them know I'm always there. It may be in the evening it may be there in the morning, but I don't go in their park.

If you get on top of a bull, he will let you know very quickly that he doesn't like you above his park. If you move down and stay on his level, he will keep talking. However, if you get on top of that sucker and start talking just a little bit aggressive, he will cut you off. He doesn't want you on top of him.

If you stay there long enough, a bull will get frustrated and tear up the earth a little bit, but more than likely he won't leave his park. You have to stay on your toes, though, because he may shut up and come stalking in quietly just to take a good look.

This is the one time of year that a bull will come into a bad sounding call. When their hormones kick in they will come to check it out no matter how bad it sounds. Early in the season, they are going to make sure it's real. If you sound real and they think you're real as you approach them, they're going to come over and take look at you.

A bull I killed two years ago on the September 7, was shot at five feet as he went by peeing on himself. I've never had any trouble getting bulls to come take a look at me.

When a bull comes in to within 60 to 80 yards, I don't use the bull call. At that stage of the game, I'm letting him know I'm the cow out in front advancing forward, and I want to check him out. If you're working with a partner, at first he's bugling behind you, acting the coward's part as if he doesn't want to come up there. See, I'm the cow and I belong to my caller. He's staying back and it's a friendly thing then, all of sudden we chirp into a different tone. We change our voice to a more aggressive tone as we move on the bull. I do my friendly cow gesture to him, then my buddy takes over with more aggressive sounds and boy that bull will lay his rack back and come over to show who's in authority.

By then, I know it is time to holster my cow call and get ready. I have pulled on bulls coming dead at me with their racks laid back and their eyes half shut. They never saw me. The bull pinpoints the source of the cow call and he knows the little bull (the caller) is squealing from back down the trail. As that bull comes in with rack laid back, he's posing. He's saying, "Look at me little bull, I'm coming over here to get you out of here I'm going to show that girl how pretty I am!"

Tag and Call

Another successful tactic you can use after the bulls have all gathered their cows is to slip along behind the herd as they come out of the feeding ground. You are going to tag along behind them. All you are going to do is call and tag, call and tag. The elk are probably going to wait for you to catch up but if they don't, use the bull call to challenge. Trick that bull into staying put or coming back to see you. Be careful if you are pushing the shooter out front. Chances are, he is going to get caught because the herd is looking and looking, back toward that caller. This happens all the time unless the guy is a really good stalker or he is working one on one. When you get two people out there, one often doesn't know where the other is.

If tagging the herd doesn't work and you know where the bull is, you can hook out and get up around him. (This only works if you are familiar with the terrain and are in good shape because you really have to get the boogie going to catch that bull!) When you get up along side the bull, get on his level and do your tending sound. As those cows pass by it doesn't matter if one blows out, or makes me and wants to bark, I do not care. I will use the bull call to make that herd bull think I am the one who threatened that cow, then I'll do an estrus mews call. That herd bull will leap right over there and try to gather me up. If it goes sour, just back off and let him go on. He will be there the next day.

Tip: Many times I will just out maneuver a bull. I start making that lovesick plead from my bull call as I move around. All of sudden things will get quiet and I know somebody is coming to check me out. If a little bull blows out, that's fine, I do not care. That big bull is going to come back there and circle down on my level and try to catch me. I don't care if he's the dominant bull or he's the satellite bull.

OK, he can't see me, things are quiet and I've played my game right. Then, that darn bull pulls back and just before he goes out of sight he is going to say something—they will always say something to you. Most guys will say something back, issue a challenge and try to make something happen again. That's just what the bull wants, he wants you to give yourself away.

You have to let him go on his way because he is going to hook around and get above you. You have to quickly move up, making calf chirp sounds, then be quiet. When the bull can't find you (in the spot you originally bugled from), he's going to head up to where he heard that calf because he knows there's a cow with that calf. He will walk right up to you. He will do it every time.

If things don't go just right when he comes in, you may have to charge him. Cow call, run right at him, bolt him out of there. This takes lots of energy, but you have to get something going. It's the last thing you can try.

Most guys are just partying along, trying to sneak and stalk and they're afraid to use their calls. They using squawking calls that don't sound right and everything goes bad in a hurry. I learned these lessons the hard way.

After The Peak Of The Rut

You will always have better luck talking to elk with your cow call later on in the season. It's tough to use a bull call then because there are so many bulls bugling, you are going to have to be one dominant son of-a-gun to challenge that big boy. Lesser bulls may run in but a dominant bull will come to check it out with his head held high, wanting to see something. He won't come in with his rack laid back peeing on himself, he comes in with a threatening posture.

You can make that lovesick bull and tending sound on your bull call, pretending you're a bull tending a cow. A bull will come in to this call with a posture that says he is so good looking. If you see one of these old bulls coming in with his rack back and eyes half closed stumbling over rocks, you know you have him.

Though the lovesick bull sound will sometimes work, if you're smart, you will use more cow calls this time of year.

The Linger Grounds

Not far from the elk bedding areas, you will find what I call the "Linger Grounds." These are good places to concentrate your efforts during the latter part of the season. They could also be called the "Fight and Linger Grounds." Everybody comes there to battle, everybody comes there to breed. Each bull may have 6 to 10 cows with him.

The linger grounds are a good place for two hunters working together. I will go up on a ridge, make sure the wind is right, and start doing my tending sounds. My partner is positioned above me talking to the bulls. One time as we were doing this, two bulls advanced only eight yards from me looking for the cow that was being tended.

In a situation like this I use a gel made from estrus urine. It is like a wax that you can rub on a piece of yarn, attach a chunk of split shot in the middle and toss it out away from you. It may take 20 to 30 minutes, but you'll bring those bulls right up by you. They're tasting with their tongues out as they come by.

This product is also available as a wick, but you have to go over the hill and set it out. With the yarn, you just flip it out there and it will hang up in a tree. I don't care if only goes six or eight yards.

Working The Bedding Areas

If you don't know the terrain, you just have to go to where you think a bull is heading. You know he will be looking for some level, wet ground for one reason, he's going to bed down. You may come to one level and two levels, then all of a sudden you can feel the refrigerator country. You've swung into that northeastern slope and there are usually elk there.

If that herd bull gets all the satellite bulls chased off and you get close, you may suddenly hear the satellite bulls bugling. (Eighty percent of bowhunters will stick a satellite bull. They never get on the big guys.) Now you may think the elk are really doing something but they're not, they're going to bed. Those satellite bulls are so fired up that they are still talking as they're leaving.

Where did they go? Usually they're just down over the hill from you. If you go too far out over that bench, they are going to smell you.

Depending on the terrain, I may hunt all day, even after the elk have bedded down. If there is a main ridge running down with several side draws coming off, I get on the ridge that's on the low side of the elk. Making sure the wind right, the draft is pulling, I try to get level with them. About mid-morning, I may roll some rocks, cow call, chirp and carry on. After that, if I hear a bunch of cows start talking in high-

This New Mexico bull scored 355 P&Y.

183   *Meline poses with his 295 P&Y Idaho bull.*

pitched sounds, I know that dominant bull has left those cows and he's coming to check me out. The herd cow has taken over. The herd figures they're getting ready to go somewhere, but they don't know where they're going. Don't pull a bugle in a situation like this. Just be patient and wait.

I love elk that take their time going to bed and I love to hear the satellite bulls spread out. Say it's 3:00 p.m. and you've napped and kept the wind in your favor. All of a sudden you give a challenge, run over 100 yards and change your voice to make a different sound. This will start things happening and if it's a decent weather day, those elk will think it's time to move. If you move down the hill doing the challenge, simulating a fight back and forth, you'll get those bulls talking and they will head for the feeding grounds early.

If you know where the herd is bedded and you don't want to go in and bother them, you can make them go to their feeding grounds earlier in the evening. If you pretend there is some action on the way to the feeding grounds, you can make it happen. This tactic works best anytime after September 15.

It's really amazing how, with the right technique, you can manipulate the behavior of a bunch of elk. One time in Idaho, we walked two and half miles below our camp down in this big canyon. We noted out across that canyon with our bull call and got five or six responses. These were ordinary sounding elk and we wanted a bigger bull.

We changed to a heavy latex on our calls and got a deep-throated, big, old sound going. All of a sudden, Mister Big answered. Everybody shut up because they knew some other big toad had showed up. Then, we changed our position, went to a different latex and simulated a battle between two bulls. After that, all those bulls started talking again.

Mister Big was down there in the black timber where he couldn't see anything. We kept talking to that old bull until finally on the fourth day he was on our front porch! He came up there to see what bull was taking care of that hillside and he brought his herd with him.

360 P&Y New Mexico Bull

I've known Tom Klumker of San Francisco River Outfitters (505-539-2517) for several years since meeting him on a New Mexico elk hunt. He kept telling me if I wanted to get away from all the people, I needed to let him take me on a hunt into the wilderness. Now I like to run around to different areas and hunt with different people, so last year I took him up on it. I put in and drew the tag.

Tom packed us to an area about 10 miles into the wilderness. We didn't see much sign going in but the terrain looked good and the map looked good. The Fish and Game said there were bulls in the area so we set up camp down in a hole. A 1,500-foot climb up a nearby hill would take us into a good-looking basin. In the basin there was a long, swamp-fed draw. That New Mexico high country has lots of water.

We made a big circle the next day and located some rub sign and some velvet sign. (Once we reached the basin, everything was filmed for my new video.) It looked like a good spot so I stepped down over the hill and put out a friendly bugle and couple of cow calls, and sprayed some scent. The second time I gave the friendly call, this big old toad answered. We learned later that particular bull would have scored about 390.

I spoke to him again, changed positions and climbed above him. I gave another bugle and before I could finish, that bull cut me off! He did not like us there. This was the day before season so we boogied way up high, staying out of the basin and slipped out of there.

We dropped off and fell into another nice pocket, looked down and there were two cows and a bull that we had spooked. (This bull turned out to be the one I eventually killed.) That was enough, we turned tail and ran out of there.

When we got down over the hill, I pulled out my map and logged the areas where we had walked. Our GPS didn't arrive in time so I was logging things on my topo as we went.

We zipped down a canyon, climbed over another ridge and dropped into a big basin. I got set up and spoke friendly along about 10:30 a.m. Another bull answered up on the hill but it looked like it was going to rain so we got out of there and went back to camp.

On opening morning, we got up and climbed back to the same spot were I got the big bull to answer. I spoke to him down off in the canyon and a little bull answered from way out on the flat. The big bull wouldn't answer. Now I didn't want that high-pitched thing so I told Clyde Johnson (my camera man), "We've got to find that big bull so let's move down country a little ways."

Checking the wind, we found we had a good draft, so we sprayed down with scent and started down. About 1/4 mile later, I stopped and gave a sweet little friendly call. All of a sudden, the big bull sounded off from up on the face of the basin! I guess he couldn't hear us from where we first called. There was no way we could move up to him so we went on out a little farther. Clyde set up the camera, hoping something might happen.

I stepped out in front of the camera, gave a little call and heard a limb pop. I looked up the hill and there came the bull that I later shot. He just came strolling down the hill and walked right out in front of me.

Above: This is a 300+ P&Y bull harvested in New Mexico.

Right: This big New Mexico bull scored a 325 P&Y.

Clyde couldn't see the bull, but he looked over and saw me all posed. The bull was about 40 yards out, checking everything and nosing the ground. Suddenly, he turned his rack and just walked off. I think he may have caught a little glimpse of Clyde.

Moving out around the elk, we cut up on the hill and made another friendly sound that was quickly answered by a high-pitched bull up on the hill. By then we had three to four bulls going and it was only the first day of season. Another shower blew in and got us wet, so for the second day in a row were back in camp by 3:00 p.m.

The next morning we went back up on the hill—same place, same exact pattern. Nothing was bugling that morning but we jumped a bull right out there in the flats. He bolted straight out of there so we moved way on out up into the big pines.

I sat down and bugled and a great big bull answered way across the canyon almost a mile way. Soon, another bull answered up on the face. I wanted to check on that big boy so we headed on a big stroll over to the face of the hill. It got real thick in there and we couldn't handle it so we just kept climbing and climbing. The sign was sparse so I suggested we head back to see if we could get some footage of the high-pitched bull. Who knows, he might be bigger than he sounded.

In order to get on top of that high-pitched bull and see what he was doing, we had to circle around and walk across a hillside. As we're walking, I'm talking friendly all the way. All of a sudden, I stopped when I thought I saw something flash down through the trees. I took out my glasses and could see it was the rack of a bull.

Clyde got the camera set up while I slipped down the hill about 12 yards in front of him. I let out some estrus cow mews and the bull got up. Down the hill he walked, popping brush and limbs as he went. He tried to grab the wind but he couldn't because it was dead, stable air.

The bull circled and headed right for me. He spoke and I answered, then dropped my cow call and readied myself for the shot. I didn't know how big this bull was but he looked pretty good walking through the trees. He came strolling right up the hill to me while Clyde filmed the whole thing. That bull walked up within eight yards of me as I hid behind a tree!

I relaxed, deciding not to shoot him because he was only about a 300. Just a nice, pretty bull. For better than 15 minutes, I played peek-a-boo with that bull. Finally, I just stepped out from behind the tree to make him leave. He raised his head turned and moved off. I stopped that bull three times as he was walking away.

Walking in front of the camera, we filmed an interview in a normal voice. We put the camera away and started to leave, but the bull continued following us. Clyde said, "What did you do to him, Abe? He's in love with you!"

We moved way up the hillside to a big canyon and found some more elk, a cow and calf and a bull. By then, we had found five bulls and hadn't covered a two square mile area.

On the third day we finally got into the big bull. We worked our way down on a bench and I played with that bull for two hours in there. He was rubbing off the velvet, beating and thumping and carrying on. There was a lot of canopy in that area and a lot of wind noise. I couldn't tell what that bull was doing in front of me. Finally, I gestured for Clyde to cut the camera. Then I gave another gesture, "I'm gonna go in and kill the dog, we'll film it later!"

Slipping on a set of Baers feet, I moved out about 30 yards in front of Clyde. He was following me but I did not know it at the time. I saw two cows advance as I stepped over a log. As I tried to get my bad leg over, somebody grabbed me and threw me down. It was Clyde. Then I heard a pop and this big bull stepped out 35 yards away with velvet hanging from his antlers. He looked at me, then looked away. I cow called, he

This rack taken from an Idaho bull scored 300+ B&C.

looked at me, groaned and walked away. We got up and couldn't find anything else before a storm blew us back to camp again.

Early the next morning after we got set up, I called and a bull answered. The camera was positioned above his seep and he was about 150 yards out from us. Tom stayed on the edge of the seep while Clyde and I shot out ahead. I was about 30 yards in front of the camera, cow calling. Tom bugled and the bull bugled. The cows went through so I estrus mewed and did some tromping sounds.

The bull stepped into view, laid back his rack and headed straight at me. That bull meant business. He was going to kick the intruder bull out of there. The way he was coming through the Christmas trees, it looked as if he was going to pass within 10 feet of me. I picked my bow out of the holster and came to full draw.

Only one thing was wrong. I had left my arrow inside my rest because I do that when I'm setting up the camera. Now I knew it was behind the rest, but I didn't care, because at 10 feet it ain't going to make any difference anyway.

Suddenly, the bull turned and headed back through the Christmas trees. I let my arrow down, popped it on my rest and drew the bow again. Swinging with the bull, I released and ran the arrow up through his flank, through his liver and out behind his shoulder. He ran out in front of Tom who gave a bugle. The bull spun around, looked at Tom and fell over. I heard a big clunk and Tom hollered, "Abe, he's down!" That bull was dead in 15 seconds after running less than 100 yards.

Abe's notes: My new video featuring this hunt will be available in January. I am putting together another feature video and a tactical video, both of which will be ready by Christmas. Ten kills are featured in the tactical video. Call 1-800-426-2417 to place your order.